Dear _____ _____ an-

Here's hoping the TITLE
of Walter's book will

JUST JESUS

not put you off. Walter
was a radical theolo-
gian- a Quaker.
I believe you both would
have liked him as I
did.
His wife, June, is
coming - I am hoping
she can meet both
of you.
Feliz año - r love-
Gretchen

JUST JESUS

MY STRUGGLE
TO BECOME
HUMAN

Walter Wink

with STEVEN E. BERRY

Foreword by JUNE KEENER WINK

IMAGE

New York

Published in the United States by Image, an imprint of the Crown
Publishing Group, a division of Random House LLC, a Penguin
Random House Company, New York.
www.crownpublishing.com

IMAGE is a registered trademark and the "I" colophon is a
trademark of Random House LLC.

Library of Congress Cataloging-in-Publication Data
Wink, Walter.
  Just Jesus : my struggle to become human / Walter Wink.—First
Edition.
     pages cm
  1. Wink, Walter. 2. Christian biography—United States. I. Title.
BR1725.W53A3 2014
  270.092—dc23
  [B]

                                                          2013037245

ISBN 978-0-307-95581-4
eBook ISBN 978-0-307-95582-1

Printed in the United States of America

Cover design by Nupoor Gordon
Cover photograph courtesy of the Estate of Walter Wink

10 9 8 7 6 5 4 3 2 1

First Edition

APRIL 1, 2010

To June:

The light of my life

The life that frees me,

That heals what wounds me,

The friend that challenges me,

Calling to me across my current

improvised soul:

I love you beyond the telling of it.

We shall not cease from exploration

And the end of all our exploring

Will be to arrive where we started

—T. S. ELIOT, *FOUR QUARTETS*

Foreword

Have you told them? Walter would look at me with an intense, anxious glance, pleading that I had already said the word. Other times, he would announce it himself: "Dementia." We both dreaded the word itself, having coped with the illness for several years. Afterward, he would soften and relax because whoever we met with would understand that he did not have to live up to the Walter Wink he once was.

And yet, throughout his illness Walter retained the core of himself, the man who loved and laughed. Oftentimes we wept together. His book was not finished. He could not die yet. Several times it seemed like he was ready to give up, but then, with new enthusiasm, the old scholar would rise up in him. Or perhaps the Holy Spirit moved him to renew his ever-present passion for giving his "last full measure of devotion"; in other words, to be an evangelist, as he liked to call himself.

Walter courageously continued to work on lectures and fulfill the invitations he had received. We moved from lecture to lecture, growing more tired but with greater determination. The last series he successfully gave were in Princeton, in Toronto, and at our local Great Barrington Quaker meeting, for the twenty-fifth anniversary of their founding. Walter felt that he needed to contribute as much as he could to the acute problem of violence, and to help people understand the Domination System and the Powers That Be.

Eventually, the Lewy Body Dementia forced him to finally stop doing workshops and lectures. He retired to his beloved garden, writing until it was no longer possible for his impoverished brain.

Each morning, we spent quiet time reading poetry, reflecting, and praying. Every spring we would reread T. S. Eliot's *Four Quartets*. Then, we would go off on a walk down one of the beautiful Berkshire trails that runs in front of our home. This became more difficult as the disease progressed, yet he seldom refused to go. Only for the last three and a half weeks of his life, he was not able to walk or get into a car.

The mornings, up until four o'clock in the afternoon, were set aside for Walter's writing. It took him years to accumulate his research and thoughts. But once he focused on putting the ideas on paper, he would go to his small study overlooking the river and then *bingo* it was finished. Sometimes when he was stuck on an idea or a word, he would walk around the house or outdoors until the problem was solved. He would rush back to his little nest and continue the task.

It was so important to him throughout his illness that he finish this book before he died. In the past, once he'd turn in a book for publication he would say, "Now I can die." In an interview, Walter once remarked about death, "I hope I live to be a ripe old age, but if I have to give my life for the gospel or justice, I hope I can do that." Writing always fulfilled that.

Just a month before he died, I asked him if he would please help me move his long, lanky, heavy legs toward the middle of the bed. He could not. I was exasperated and explained in a louder voice, "I am really getting irritated. Can't you help at all?" He could not.

Afterward, I moved to the head of the bed to tuck him in with hugs and a kiss good night, when he said in a clear voice, "Open up your heart and let God's love come in." I was shocked because he had not been able to speak at all by that time. His speech had deteriorated to a mumble. My reaction was to sing his words loud, then soft, then high, then low, over and over, until we both burst out laughing.

Even today, I still sing our little song, "Open up your heart and let God's love come in."

—*June Keener Wink, June 2013*

Preface

After a Jesus Seminar banquet in Sonoma, California, a colleague and I decided a walk would do us good. So we headed in the direction of the motel where he was staying. As we went, we began discussing how a person's personal history affects one's scholarship. Just knowing people's religious backgrounds, for example, helped us understand comments they make in the Seminar.

We concluded that someone ought to do a volume in which the authors of the outstanding books on Jesus are invited to write an autobiography of their interest in Jesus. Perhaps if we all knew the others' stories, we would have more respect, understanding, and compassion for each other. We could be pretty caustic with each other, myself no less than others. As a test case, my colleague and I told our own stories. We arrived at the motel far too soon, so we swung around the corner and took in a prodigiously long block. Time after time, we came to the motel and again turned the corner until the night had worn down and our stories were told.

"An autobiography of my interest in Jesus," perhaps that is too ambitious. What I have done here is far less grand. I have simply written down vignettes, or excerpts of my life's story that I find interesting. These autobiographical reflections are in no way exceptional. Everyone has a life story. Some are more interesting than others, but they all deserve a hearing. My story may, at the very least, show why I theologically think the way that I do.

How does my autobiography affect my interpretation of Scripture? How has my theology come out of my experiences?

JUST JESUS

When did I first begin to want to become more human, and when did I realize that Jesus was the key to my becoming? My faith was quite simple and direct. It was just Jesus. I wanted to know who this Jesus really is. The church was my refuge; I learned about Jesus and, by his example, I saw how to live. His example of how to live opened up a new freedom that was felt, if not articulated. For those who identify themselves as Christians, as I do, Jesus is the author of our humanity, and the goal of this book is the humanization of Jesus. I feel like I am in a rhetorical fistfight to humanize religion through Jesus's pragmatism. I can offer the reader no definition of what humanizing entails. Each person's journey is unique, an act of creation.

THE BIBLE AS PUNISHMENT

My first vivid encounter with Jesus took place in the fourth grade, when I was expelled from Sunday school for rowdiness. My parents punished me by making me skip Sunday dinner and stay in my room. For my comfort, my mother handed me the Revised Standard Version (RSV) of the New Testament, which had just been published. I began at the beginning, with the long list of somebody who was the father of somebody, and somebody who was the father of somebody else, and on and on. The further I read, the more fascinated I became. Here is the most important book in the world, I thought, and yet it doesn't make any sense. Why begin a book with this long list of ancestors? Thus my curiosity about Scripture was first piqued. Imagine, punishment by reading a Bible! My mother may not have been seeking to punish me after all, but to guide me to deeper life meanings through Scripture. Yet there are people who use the Bible to bludgeon others on a daily basis.

HEALTH

It is said that "It's a good life—if you've got your health." But it snuck up on me: first, twenty years of restless leg syndrome (RLS), then prostate cancer (in remission), then pneumonia (healed), then dementia (fatal). I had always thought that a life-threatening illness or accident would force me to attend to my relationship with God in the absence of real commitment. In fact, the deeper I slipped into the darkness, the less I cared about God. Prayer was out of the question. In my journal, I once scribbled: "If I have a soul, it's silent. I don't know what the point of this book is anymore. If God won't heal me, God can go hang." My helpers tried everything to bring me back to my relationship with God.

In my early twenties, my personal demand for perfection escalated infinitely. If my father could demand perfection to the extent of inspecting every blade of grass on the fresh-mowed lawn, then how much more could God expect? There was always this possibility of not living up to what God wanted of me. It led to a massive denial because I couldn't own up to who I really was. And to tell the truth about myself would be to divulge my innermost self, leading to rejection by God and others. For that reason, I couldn't make eye contact with people lest they see into my true heart. You can imagine what a relief it was to discover that the "wrath of God" was not divine retribution for our sins, but rather divine forbearance, whereby God "gives us up" to the consequences of our folly (Rom. 1:18–32), of which global warming is only one of many.

My deepest fear, however, was that I could no longer address this global mess that surrounds us every day. I had felt so strongly that God had called me to help others find meaning in life, but now the best I could do was to give whatever my leftover self could offer. I felt like I was letting God down when I didn't use the gifts given me. And so I was afraid that I was a fraud. I had a hard time being aware of the reality of God.

I was afraid that restless leg syndrome and all the medications blindly thrown at it had permanently damaged my brain. And memory loss led to acute daily failures in speaking and writing, which prevented me from believing in myself. I had to cancel all workshops, which felt like amputation without anesthesia. And so I spiraled down into depression and a night I had never known before, experiencing nearly all the side effects announced on the pharmacists' disclaimers. This was more than RLS, though it was that too. Finally a doctor recognized the symptoms: it was a form of dementia, an acute memory disorder that eventually proves fatal but can, with proper care, be delayed. And now, thank God, medications have been developed that are effective for the relief of RLS symptoms and for dementia. I was told that I would never lecture or lead workshops again, but I can write, and even have recently lectured in a limited way.

Then this bombshell: I had not turned my back on God. I hadn't lost my faith. I was being poisoned to death. On July 21, 2007, the makers of OxyContin (Oxycodone hydrochloride) were assessed a $634.5 million fine for failing to warn the public about the painkiller's risk of addiction and death. OxyContin had already caused 146 deaths and had contributed to another 318 deaths—*with the full knowledge of the pharmaceutical executives.* I feel certain that I would soon have died had my family not gotten me off the drug immediately. So I hadn't lost my faith. It was stolen from me. It was a new form of unbelief: "chemical atheism."

In the meantime, I do jigsaw puzzles and other memory exercises, walk forty minutes a day, work out with a trainer at a gym, do stretching and weights daily, receive neurofeedback on an experimental basis, and ride an elliptical machine before bed. I enjoy life, sleep better, and have even accepted an invitation to give a lecture in the spring.

The defining event of my childhood took place when I was nine years old. When I was a child, I lied quite often out of fear of my father's wrath. One day when he came home from work, he asked me if I had put my bike in the garage. I answered yes, and ran out to the front yard to put it away. It was gone. I ran into the house shouting that my bike had been stolen. "Where was it?" Dad asked. "In the front yard," I naïvely replied. "I thought you said it was in the garage," he said. It was entrapment; he had hidden it himself.

After dinner that night, he and my mother convened a trial at the kitchen table where I stood before the bar of justice, being judged. They found me guilty of being a liar, and gave me two choices: to leave home for good, or to spend the night in the "brig" (a garage storeroom). Sensing that my life in my family was over, I opted to leave. They asked me to whom I planned to go. I said I would go live with my Aunt Sue and Uncle Dave. "Oh no, they wouldn't want a liar living with them." Then I suggested the preacher's son, who was my best friend. But every suggestion met with the same refrain: "Oh, no, they wouldn't want a liar living with them." There appeared to be no alternative to the brig. It must have been fall. I can still remember the sound of the pecan tree being lashed by the wind.

After a while Dad came to the door and told me it was time to turn off the light. I was terrified. Now I was in total darkness, inside and out. Whatever hope I still had disappeared. Only years later, after my parents had died, my sister told me that she had been at her bedroom window, keeping watch, unable to do anything about it. My mother must have been devastated. She had to have known this was all wrong. She was Phi Beta Kappa, a prolific reader, and a person of compassion. But she had been taught to obey her husband. She must have finally been unable to take it any longer. Somehow she must have persuaded him to release me from their "jail." It seemed like hours. It could as well have been eternity.

That night in a very profound sense I "died" emotionally.

The next afternoon I met Dad in the yard. "Do you still love me?" he asked.

"No," I answered.

"Will you obey me?"

"Yes," I replied. And I did.

BOY SCOUTS

I was inducted into the Order of the Arrow as a child, a society of Boy Scouts who were trained in ecological awareness and survival skills that was premised on the love of nature. The climax of the ritual was an all-night silent vigil in the woods, with only a dull sheath knife and a canteen of water. I was directed to keep a fire going all night long and not sleep. There was no fear; I was alone in a place I loved to be the most. Turtle doves serenaded me the live-long night. That experience stands as emblematic of many times in my life when solitude and nature provided emotional comfort.

Together, my liberal Methodist church and the Boy Scouts formed a surrogate family that compensated, at least in part, for the alienation I felt from my natural family. Every summer, my experience of God in nature went deeper.

PRAYER FOR WRITING

On this beautiful end of summer day, Lord, I bring my whole self, including my ambivalence to you, and offer myself to be used by you in the writing of this book. Deliver me from egocentric plots. Give me courage to rewrite to perfection. I do commit myself to you, O God, in life, in death. I commit myself to the truth. I will not be cowed by pain or use it as an excuse for resistance. I will try to hold myself open to the depths. I ask for images and metaphors to flow when I write. I ask for help in revising my book, to make it really readable. I ask for patience to do it right.

I woke up this morning so happy because I had slept all night. I feel like I ought to be writing, but I don't have the energy. June urges me to enjoy whatever I am doing, whether grocery shopping or a workout—that too is living. I don't have to write this book. All these mundane tasks are just as important as writing this book. And I should be so grateful for these moments. When I *want* to write, that will the right time.

THE SON OF THE MAN[*]

We have plundered the ecosystem as if there were no end to its fecundity. It is far from clear that human beings will survive. Already millions have died, many at the hands of fellow humans. Our leaders have failed to act while they could. The apocalyptic scenarios in which the biblical "son of man" appears to judge the nations are terrifyingly vivid. But there is another alternative, in which the Human Being will reveal itself to us as nonviolent, and by some miracle we will awaken to the crisis and act. Against all hope, apartheid and the Berlin Wall fell. Quite literally, our task today is to save this crippled and crying world.

There are few mysteries in biblical studies as unfathomable as the expression "the son of the man." Scarcely any topic in all research has received more attention with less result. Here are the few facts that define the problem. "Son of man" (without definite articles) appears one hundred and eight times in the Hebrew Bible Scriptures, ninety-three of them in Ezekiel. Curiously, God refuses to call

* Previously published in Walter Wink, *The Human Being: Jesus and the Enigma of the Son of the Man* (Minneapolis, MN: Fortress Press, 2001).

Ezekiel by his given name, but addresses him only as "son of man." No one else calls Ezekiel "son of man," only God. A similar expression appears in the New Testament some eighty-seven times, all but three in the Gospels, and curiously, eighty-four times on the lips of Jesus and no one else.

"The son of *the* man" is so awkward that virtually all translators omit the second definite article. You may be wondering why I use the Greek expression in the Gospels, "the son of the man." Quite simply, I do so because that is what the Greek phrase says, and it should be translated that way, despite a conspiracy of translators to render it with only one definite article, "the son of man." To add insult to injury, they also add caps where there are none. I will translate the expression literally, with both articles, to underscore its oddness and crudity. I apologize on behalf of the New Testament for the double sexism in this expression. I will do everything in my power to counteract it.

Herein lies the puzzle: Jesus apparently avoided designation as messiah, son of God, or God, though these titles were given to him after his death and resurrection by his disciples. But Jesus is repeatedly depicted as using the obscure expression "the son of the man" as virtually his only form of self-reference. Yet, his disciples, after his death, almost completely ignored the expression. Paul never once used it, nor any of the writers of the other epistles. It appears only a few times in the writing of the Apostolic Fathers. So far as we know, no one worshipped "the son of the man" or made that figure the one addressed in prayer. Insofar as the expression was used by the later church, it was merely fused with the other Christological titles, or treated as an expression indicating Jesus's human nature, as opposed to his divine nature. "The son of the man" was never made the basis of any church confession, never appeared in any of the church's creeds, and, in time, virtually disappeared from usage except in Gnostic circles.

It is at least clear that Jesus did not use "the son of the man" as a self-deprecating expression of humility. If there is anything Jesus was not, it was modest. Few people ever spoke with such unmediated authority, or made a higher claim, than Jesus that he was ushering the Reign of God into the world. "Son of" is simply a Semitic idiom meaning "pertaining to the following genus or species." Thus "son of the quiver" is an arrow (Lam. 3:13), a "son of the herd" is a calf (Gen. 18:7), and a "son of the night" refers to something one night old (Jon. 4:10). Joshua and Zerubbabel are "sons of oil," that is, anointed ones (Zech. 4:14), and a "son of wisdom" is a wise person (Isa. 19:11). Hence "son of man" simply means "man," or "human being." This idiom is used in scores of ways in the Hebrew Bible, and it is never translated literally ("son of"), but it is always rendered into an equivalent English expression.

Always, that is, except for one important exception: the phrase "son of man." Idiomatically, it simply means "human being." But the pressure of theological reflection surrounding Jesus's use of the expression has caused translators to leave the phrase in its confusing idiomatic form. The more recent translations of the Hebrew Bible Scripture are now rendering the expression in good English: "mere man" or "mortal man" (Today's English Version, or TEV), "a human being" or "O man" (Revised English Bible, or REB), "mortal(s)" or "the one" (New Revised Standard Version, or NRSV). But even these versions still persist in translating "son of man" literally when they come to the New Testament.

When I was about ten years old, I wanted to drive the car. I hounded Dad until he reluctantly gave in. I got in the driver's seat and he slipped into the passenger's side. I started the motor and let out the clutch. Down the hill we sped, right at the garage. In panic, I forgot which pedal was the brake. Dad reached over to put on the brake, but his heel hit the accelerator just when I popped the clutch. Remorselessly, the car went straight through the garage and plowed through the brick rear wall, which finally stopped us. Neighbors gathered upon hearing the noise. Dad couldn't admit to letting me do such a thing as drive, so he took the blame.

He was very calm; never did he raise his voice. I was left to stack the bricks. A few years later as a sophomore in high school, I cleaned the bricks of their mortar and laid them. Each day when he got home from the office, he inspected the bricks I'd cleaned that day and redid the ones he decided were not perfect. And I mean *perfect*. In time, I became a pretty good bricklayer. I felt this was Dad's revenge, but I agreed that I deserved it so I couldn't voice my frustration and anger.

My deep perfectionism did not arise from any form of indoctrination from fundamentalism. It came straight out of my desperate desire to win my parents'—and God's—love. Though I intellectually knew that God loved me, I was unable to fully internalize that message. As a compensation for my sense of lovelessness, I sought every honor and pursued every election I could find. But the more I succeeded, the more bittersweet the reward. What I really wanted was divine election, as in Judaism and Calvinism. What I wanted was unconditional love from God.

WOUNDS IN OUR EXISTENCE

There still remains a wound at the core of my existence. Why did I have to struggle so hard to overcome its consequences? I know this: without that wound, I would have become a shallow caricature of a person. Sins, unattended, come out of our wounds. More so, our wounds provide the characteristic style of our sinning. I am not tempted by money. Drop a pile of money at my feet and I would simply turn it in. But relationships are another story. I ask myself, what did my wound teach me about God? How did it shape my theology? Is it not true that my wound was the source of whatever compassion I possess? How did God use my wound to heal me? There is an ancient Greek saying that runs:

> *God sends the wound.*
> *God is wounded.*
> *God is the wound.*
> *God heals the wound.*

I have struggled mightily with the idea that God sends wounds. Did God send *my* wound, I wondered. I understood that God worked for my healing through it, but did the initial wounding come from God? If I want to give God credit for the healing, does God get the credit for the pain? Must I say that the Holy Spirit sent my neuroses in order to facilitate dealing with my darkness? Why this face, that illness, that body, those parents, this nationality, that ethnicity? Must I *forgive God* for the grievances of my existence?

Millions of children have suffered far more trauma than I. No matter, for a child, wounds are absolute. It is not the degree of trauma we go through that determines trauma, but how it has altered our lives. My father should have protected me. The harmless lies of a little boy scarcely warranted such a draconian response. What he did was inexcusable. No father who sets up a child to fail is loving. But these wounds provided whatever strengths I had as a person. Mom's intellectualism and Dad's discipline were my greatest gifts from them, even though they further damaged me in the process. Without Mom pushing me, I could never have become a scholar. And without Dad's uncompromising sense of ethics and morality, I might have wasted my youth on trivial things. All my honors in high school and college—and they were considerable—were compensations for my conviction that I was unlovable.

For most of my life I refused to forgive Dad. I yearned for his apology, but it never came. When he finally took his own life, I was initially angry. He had robbed me of the last chance for us to be reconciled in this life. Later, I saw it as an act of love. As I look back now, I realize that fathers in that day did not have the tools to handle their feelings or those of their children. I was first able to *feel* that my parents really did love me just months before Mom died. I was deeply moved to see them holding hands at the bus station.

It would be the last time I would see my mother alive. Over time, I realized that they just made a tragic mistake, and my refusal to love and forgive them had robbed all of us of much deserved happiness. With that understanding, my resistance to forgiveness crumbled.

But I still struggle to become a human being. The hardest struggles are with God. I was a child who had been told by those closest to me that it was not possible to be human. At some point, I renounced trying to be good and instead chose to be real.

SINGIN' THE BLUES

One of the things I find most helpful during dark days is singing the Blues. At first I chanted Psalms, either biblical Psalms or ones I put together. But I tried too hard, and they got all tangled up with my perfectionism. So my spiritual guide, Andy Canale, had me create the Blues on the spot, with no art or craft to spoil the spontaneity of the songs. Andy taught me not to fight the Blues. They are among the best tools we have to counter the Powers. The slaves knew that. When there is no conceivable hope, singing the Blues opens up a new and other reality. It reminds us that we can choose the reality we want to occupy. It doesn't have to be pretty. It can be a single note. Once you are acclimated with the Psalms, try singin' the Blues. You can write them at first, and then wing it. Andy and I alternated lines; June and I tend to repeat the person lining out the lyrics. The worse, the better. Here is an example of the doggerel we produced:

> *I'm sad,*
> *makes me mad,*
> > *I can't even write this letter.*
> *I wail and cry*
> *Fit to die*
> > *And insist that I deserve better.*

How 'bout you, God?
I know it's odd,
> *But do you ever sing the Blues?*
We can sing them together
In all kinds of weather
> *Suffering is how we pay our dues.*
I guess you're hurt
when I treat you like dirt.
> *Still, you haven't given up on me.*
Your love was there
But I didn't much care
> *blinded so I just couldn't see.*

Recently, my wife and I discovered another relief for the terrors of the night: singing Christmas carols. Not the soupy ones, but the old standards. Every time June would sing and chant, I experienced immediate relief. With astonishing success, singing carols alleviates nightmares, circular dreams, and sleepwalking. I have learned to accept my depression and work with it. Often, I need lots of help.

The Human Being keeps us going. There is no guarantee that someone else will respond to singing the Blues or Christmas carols, but it certainly has helped me. I discovered that I don't have as much depression when I stop running away from the Blues all the time. Is it possible that my restless legs want, not to run away, but to dance? The Human Being is somehow fed by strange behaviors, and I received a palpable benefit from them. As Andy put it, I was being challenged to live my own exegesis.

RACISM AND INJUSTICE
IN THE EYES OF A CHILD

I couldn't have been older than six years when I befriended
a black boy who was about my age and lived in "servants'
quarters" down the alley. We played, undisturbed, in the
segregated city of Dallas, Texas. That alley was our turf.
One Christmastide, the older boys in the neighborhood
gathered and stacked all of the used Christmas trees into a
big pile on an empty lot across the street. I thought it would
be a beautiful sight burning—this was during my pyroma-
niac phase. When no one else was left but my friend and
me, I lit the pyre. It was pretty all right; the flames threatened five houses! We filled our tiny buckets with water at
my house and ran across the street, tossing the remainder
on the fire, and then ran back. Soon, adults were everywhere. Where were those kids?

The fire marshal fished us out from under my bed and
gave us a verbal thrashing. But something was wrong.
He was blaming my friend, and it had been my idea to
light the trees. The fire marshal just wouldn't listen. He
assumed that it was the fault of the little black kid. My
parents would not let me play with him anymore. My
genuine repentance was mingled with moral outrage
such as only little kids can voice. That day I discovered

something of what racism is. It just wasn't fair. How fortunate I was to have had this experience, so that when the Civil Rights Movement came along, I already had in my body a visceral reaction to the mistreatment of people of color.

FIRST ACT OF CIVIL DISOBEDIENCE

Around 1940, I decided to go for a swim on the way home from school with two friends, Bobby and Ham. I had learned to swim underwater the summer before, so Bobby and I took long dives at the deepest place. I was in the middle of the pond, about fifteen feet deep, when I suddenly realized I had forgotten how to swim! I reached for Bobby, grabbed him, and down we went together. I let go of him, we bobbed to the surface, he pushed me toward the dam, I grabbed him, we went down, I let go, and he pushed me toward the dam, on and on. Ham just watched. At last we reached the dam, crawled on, and lay there coughing the water out of our lungs. Now it so happened that Bobby was Jewish. And my parents had discovered that Bobby cussed and was therefore deemed a bad influence. But Bobby had just recently saved my life! So, in an early exercise in civil disobedience, I simply ignored them and went on playing with him.

In high school during the early 1950s, six of us seniors piled into an old station wagon loaned to us by one of the kids' parents and lit out on a five-state barnstorming tour, camping all the way. We had written a play on good citizenship called "The Americaneers," which we would perform for obliging Rotary, Kiwanis, and Lions Clubs, and anyone else that would have us. The centerpiece of the trip was a hiking expedition of Philmont Scout Ranch in New Mexico, and then off we went to do our play again, in Colorado, Kansas, and Oklahoma, winding up in Texas. It was exhilarating to experience the country this way.

During that stage in my life, though, I was a naïve conservative devotee of religious nationalism. America was the context through which I understood the Bible. As I grew older, I couldn't help but notice the discrepancy between the gospel of love I had learned in church, the delusions of imperialism, and the sheer evil of racism. It felt as if my Americanism was being challenged.

These questions were further incited by a small journal for youth published by Methodists. In one issue, the centerfold featured an article about pacifism on the left side and a discourse on prayer on the right. At that point, my belief in the Bible and belief in America, a country that had just heroically returned from war and was embarking on another, were inextricably woven together. That juxtaposition of peace and prayer helped me to see outside of myself, and sums me up even to this day (though I would substitute "practitioner of active nonviolence" for "pacifism").

SOUTHERN METHODIST UNIVERSITY

I remember in my senior year at Southern Methodist University (SMU), I was president of the Texas students' consortium of colleges and universities. At the same time my lifelong buddy, Richard Deats, was the student body president of SMU. Neither of these sham organizations had a sense of purpose. So we decided to stir the pot by calling for the racial integration of the fraternities and permitting communists to teach. Mind you, this was the heart of the McCarthy era.

One night, at 2:45 a.m., the phone rang. The caller gave his name and said he was the president of the student council at Oklahoma University, in Dallas, for the Texas/Oklahoma game. I had never heard of him. We conversed quite civilly for a time about my views on integration. As we prepared to sign off I said, "By the way, the president of the Oklahoma student council is Graham Funderburk," and hung up. A few minutes later the phone rang, and a chorus of voices shouted obscenities at me.

It was the summer of my nineteenth year that I left my home in Dallas to work in an Oregon lumber mill. Without any friends, thrown back on my own collapsed spiritual resources, I found myself one afternoon in a forest of virgin Douglas fir. At their feet were rhododendrons fifteen feet tall, in full bloom. Previously, such a sight would have filled me with adoration of God, for the beauty of nature had always been my most immediate avenue to Him. But now I felt totally alienated from what I once held so dearly. If there was no God, there was no one to thank for the glories of nature, no way to commune with God through nature, no Other to meet me in the things that He has made. I tried reading my pocket Revised Standard Version (RSV) of the New Testament. Randomly, I opened to the Book of Acts. The more I read, the more alienated I felt. The Holy Spirit poured out on the disciples' healings—none of it seemed possible. Either the whole thing was a lie, or at least most of it, or else my world was a lie, or at least part of it.

In high school, my dentist had asked me what I planned to do with my life. I'd already checked out the Forest Service and set it aside. With his fistful of tools in my mouth, I managed to croak out, "a psychologist."

He shot back, "Why don't you become a super-psychologist?"

"What's that?" I mumbled.

"A minister."

Something clicked inside me. I knew with absolute certainty that God had called me to the ministry. Even during my atheistic phase, which, as many do, I felt profoundly throughout college, I knew that the God whom I no longer believed in was still calling me to the ministry. I can still remember visiting my girlfriend's church, desperately seeking my childhood religion, with nothing to put in its place. The pastor read Matthew 6:25–34, a passage from the Sermon on the Mount:

> Therefore I tell you, do not worry about your life, what you will eat or what you will drink, or about your body, what you will wear. Is not life more than food, and the body more than clothing? Look at the birds of the air; they neither

sow nor reap nor gather into barns, and yet your heavenly Father feeds them. Are you not of more value than they? And can any of you by worrying add a single hour to your span of life? And why do you worry about clothing? Consider the lilies of the field, how they grow; they neither toil nor spin, yet I tell you, even Solomon in all his glory was not clothed like one of these. But if God so clothes the grass of the field, which is alive today and tomorrow is thrown into the oven, will he not much more clothe you—you of little faith? Therefore do not worry, saying, 'What will we eat?' or 'What will we drink' or 'What will we wear?' For it is the Gentiles who strive for all these things; and indeed your heavenly Father knows that you need all these things. But strive first for the kingdom of God and God's righteousness, and all these things will be given to you as well.

Suddenly it struck me: this passage is falsifiable. I can put it to an empirical test. Rather than simply doubting God's existence, I will make a trial of it. I will commit the coming summer to putting this promise to a scientific test. I will behave as if it were true. Then I will know whether there is a God or not.

After World War II, it seemed like everyone was out of work. I had lost my job at the lumber mill in Oregon due to an industry-wide strike. But I had joined up with a couple of guys, one of whom had a car. We decided to go to Crater Lake, just for fun, and got jobs picking strawberries. It was no good—$1.25 for a ten-hour day. We slept in the Eugene Town Dump.

About this time I received a letter from a religious woman who asked me what I intended to do next, and I said that I didn't know where to go. She told me that she owned a sawmill that was not on strike (typical: Christian non-unionized shop), and if there was a place, I had a job. She and her companion offered to drop me off in Salem on their way to Portland, and it seemed the only logical conclusion.

As we entered the town, though, she asked if I'd mind if they stopped to see an old friend. He was the head of the Chamber of Commerce. She asked him if anybody was hiring. He replied, "Well, Carl Hoge is having a sale at his furniture store; maybe he could use a hand." Just then the doorbell rang, and in walked Carl. Yes, he needed someone to restock furniture and be janitor. I had a job.

Now that I was in Salem with a job, I needed a place to stay. I saw a house with a sign on the porch: "Rooms."

Some little voice inside me said, *This is it!* The male owner was watering the lawn. I went up to him and said, "I have to stay here." He said he was sorry but they were all full. "That's impossible!" I blurted out. "Could you go look? Maybe someone moved out overnight." Well, he said, he could look, but he was pretty sure that they were full.

Just then his wife came out on the porch. I hailed her, saying I had to stay there. She said there was nothing, unless I would be willing to sleep on a cot on the basement landing. I took it. She hung a bedspread for privacy and gave me a lawn chair by the furnace. The following morning the landlady came walking down the basement stairs as I sat in the lawn chair. Without even turning her head toward me, she announced, "God has sent you here to receive the gift of the Holy Spirit." That's all she said.

This was in 1954, several years before the earliest beginnings of the "Charismatic movement." I knew nothing about the Holy Spirit, only what I had read in Acts. But here I was, sharing a home with very kind fundamentalists, eager to share their faith. The Irish washerwoman in town decided that my baptism by sprinkling was inadequate. So she and other believers from her house gathered around the second-floor bathtub to "do it right." They filled the tub and I got in, wearing only my swimming suit, struggling with how to get all six foot three inches of me submerged entirely. For when they pushed down my head, my knees popped up. When they pushed down my knees, my head popped up. Down went the head, up came the knees. I began to giggle. Soon I was convulsively laughing. God must have split His sides bellowing in counterpoint!

THE PENTECOSTAL CHURCH
from July 22, 1954

Imagine me in a room full of people all singing choruses—simple sincere songs—about us and Christ. The people all have their eyes shut, singing in prayer, some clapping, some reaching their arms up, yearning with all their hearts to have more of Jesus. Over on the side is a piano, a bass fiddle, and an accordion. As we stood singing suddenly my fingers began to burn, tingle as if they'd gone to sleep. But they weren't! Circulation was unhindered. This burning spread to my arms. I wanted to lift my arms to him [Jesus], but pride held me back, and now pride chained my arms to my sides. Not thwarted, the tingling ecstasy spread to my knees, my feet, and my back. It was as if some power had shot me through with electricity, as if I were part of a huge power line a foot in diameter. I couldn't stand it! It was like nothing I'd ever felt before. I was crushed to my seat, mystified, confused—and still the echo of the tingling remained. I knew that something Real, something more powerful than dynamite had been playing over me.

Then the minister rose and said, "Let's worship the Lord." On all sides, people started singing, saying, "Praise the Lord," "Hallelujah," "Thank you Jesus," making up the music as they went on. Then one of the strangest experiences I've ever witnessed happened. People began prophesying and speaking in tongues.

The most important thing is what happened after the service. At the close we'd risen again to worship the Lord, and the power of God was so strong in that group that it cascaded from heart to heart like pounding surf. Again I felt that strange, overpowering tingling. I was dimly aware that the service was over, that those who desired to could stay and pray, but I couldn't move. I was knotted by conflict. One minister said, "Somehow I feel that there is someone in this room tonight for whom God has something special." As I was still under the surge of this electrical tension one of the preachers came up to me, took my hand, and asked me if I was ready to serve the Lord no matter where it led me. When I murmured yes, he led me to the platform. Then the three ministers stood around me as I knelt, praising God and speaking in tongues, and raising the most glorious din I'd ever heard. Suddenly all my fears, pride, doubt, all my holdouts slipped away. It was just God and I, and the praising was a barrier to keep all else out.

Now the Power pulsing through my blood, my nerves, increased. My feet burned, tingled, as did my hands. Suddenly my legs were touched by heat. It spread. (This was all the physical reaction. Actually this is dimly remembered, as my central consciousness was with Jesus in Paradise. That's all I sought. The rest—just happened to me.) I remember the glorious release as, kneeling, I stretched my hands to God. Then I remember being on my feet. Then I felt myself falling backward as I stretched deeper and deeper into the burning light, as all my flesh throbbed with the wind of his passing. They caught me, but I didn't care. I was in Jesus's hands. I went down perfectly relaxed and lay there.

Then the Power increased yet more. Now single spots were touched—my neck at the throat, my back, my tongue, my head, and always my hands, my feet. A preacher said, "Praise Him, open your mouth." And suddenly I found myself singing, stronger, stronger still, making up melodies in complete release, complete abandon, complete love. Then I spoke a little in tongues, but fear held me back. I didn't believe in it, you see. I sang, and sang, and praised God. Then I was swept with such joy that I began laughing where I lay. Still I tingled. Then the waves subsided. . . .

SPLIT IN TWO

When I returned to Southern Methodist University in the fall, and tried to share this experience with my friends, all but two thought I had flipped out: Virginia, my first wife, and the Presbyterian chaplain. I had never felt so sane. In some ways, however, the experience threatened to split me into halves. Even now I feel a twinge of embarrassment at my nineteen-year-old exuberance. One split was between reason and experience; another was between spirit and sex. I couldn't stomach Pentecostal fundamentalism. I had, after great struggle, offered my intellect to God, and had the very clear sense that God had handed it back, with the injunction to use it for God rather than for my own ego. Those instructions said nothing about making a sacrifice of my intellect.

So now, with very little help from church or seminary, and from only a few friends, I was faced with the arduous task of trying to integrate this concussive experience with the rest of my life, and to figure out how to think about it in the context of science, history, politics, psychology, and theology. That journey has been long and exhilarating, and I am grateful to those who have mentored me through it thus far.

The pastor of my church in Dallas, from my first awareness until I entered college, was Dr. Marshall T. Steel, a graduate of Union Theological Seminary in New York City. In a political climate that was extremely conservative, Dr. Steel was a highly diplomatic and cautious advocate of the United Nations and racial integration. His whole theology was "the Fatherhood of God and the Brotherhood of Man." He never abused us by threats of hellfire and damnation. I was untouched by fundamentalist strictures until I went to Oregon that summer. I never heard the Pauline message, though I came to treasure it. I was totally unfamiliar with the terms "grace" and "justification." I was just a Methodist perfectionist, steeped in the Sermon on the Mount, convinced that my hope was to achieve the perfection demanded of me by Scripture.

Our worldviews determine to a large extent what we can believe about life, faith, and the very cosmos. If we are unaware of what worldviews have claimed our allegiance, they will determine our behavior in ways to which we are simply blind. At a far deeper level than ideologies or myths, worldviews tend to dictate what we are able to believe. They are not just the presuppositions by which we think, but the very foundation of thought itself. Consequently, people who have difficulty believing in prayer, or spiritual healing, or the life of the spirit, or God, are, in my experience, suffering far more from a worldview problem than a theological problem.

Worldviews provide a picture of the nature of things: where is heaven, where is earth, what is visible and what is invisible, what is real and what is unreal. As I am using the term "worldviews," they are not philosophies, theologies, or even myths or tales about the origin of things. We might think of our worldview as the foundation of the house of our minds. On that foundation we erect the walls and roof, which are the myths we live by, the symbolic understandings of our world. The furnishings—the stuff to sit on, lie down on, and eat with—are our theologies and personal philosophies. People notice the sofa and rugs (our theologies), they comment on the structure (the key myths), but few notice the foundation (our worldview). It is covered, hidden from view. In the very act of opposing another person's thought, we usually share the same worldview.

The slogan that many clergy were taught in seminaries was: "Science tells us *how* the world was created, theology tells us *why*." This is slick, but it is basically a materialistic view of reality. This "how" and "why" distinction is spurious; as Bruce Bradshaw points out, science and religion ask different kinds of "why" questions, such as: What are the processes that have made the creation possible? Or, What is the role of evolution in biological emergence? Instead, science serves religion by focusing on the intermediate "why" questions, such as: What are the processes and systems that are required in order to create a world? The answers to these intermediate questions shed light on the ultimate "why" questions, such as: Why did Adam and Eve rebel against God when the "garden" was paradisiacal? What is the role of myth in theological thought? What are the purposes of God in the creation of the world?

The price paid for this uneasy truce with science was the loss of a sense of the whole and the loss of the unity of heavenly and earthly aspects of existence. Science and religion cannot be separated. The heavens and the earth reveal the glory of God, and it is the divine vocation of scientists to uncover the majesty of God.

When I returned to Southern Methodist University after my summer in Oregon, I came to the conclusion that there had to be a God. But there was no content. I said the word

"God," and something resonated as true, but I had abandoned my childhood faith and had not arrived at anything else. As a college "intellectual," I had made reason my God. I was unaware that I had accepted a materialistic worldview, and that my doubts were, in fact, the consequence of trying to embrace two antithetical worldviews simultaneously. Once I came to understand this, I could affirm that the real God is the actual creator of the real world.

Southern Methodist University was only a mile from my home, and I had lived at home all through university, so it was time to move out. I jumped at the chance to attend Union Theological Seminary in New York City, a move that should have greatly pleased my mother. I was further encouraged by Pastor Marshall T. Steel, who was an alumnus. Union was arguably the premier seminary in the world when I was there, and I caught the fading glimmer of that greatness. I had the pleasure of being taught by Reinhold Niebuhr, James Muilenburg, Wilhelm Pauck, Cyril Richardson, W. D. Davies, John Macquarrie, Samuel Terrien, and George W. (Bill) Webber, among others. I particularly found Niebuhr's stress on sin too negative. I kept asking, was there space for the Holy Spirit, grace, spiritual healing? Here I showed my colors as a true Wesleyan Methodist—not a popular position in the neo-orthodox climate of Union.

GANGS IN NEW YORK

As a seminary student, I had a "field work" assignment at a church just north of Columbia-Presbyterian Hospital. I had about twelve high school kids in a Methodist Youth Fellowship class. They were initially skeptical about me, but when I showed up in a lumberjack outfit they began to warm to me. They were a ragtag bunch.

Some of them had been in the Jester gang, while others just tried to keep out of their way. When I arrived, the gang members were demoralized over the death of one of their number in a "rumble" with the Egyptian Kings at Highbridge Park. He had polio and couldn't flee when the rest of his buddies split. At that point, more Jesters joined our church. Over time, our diverse group began to meld and took a genuine interest in theology, especially non-violence.

At one meeting, Willy confided to me that he had quit the Jesters and had therefore been challenged to a fight by the head of the gang. You didn't just quit a gang—you had to fight your way out. Willy was not afraid, but he felt that his new faith prohibited violence. He wanted to know whether I thought fighting was wrong. I discussed it without offering an opinion about what he should do.

During the next meeting I asked Willy what had happened. He said that he met his opponent in the park. Each had a second to keep it "clean." When they faced each other, Willy said to the gang leader: "It takes more courage to refuse to fight than to fight. I'm not going to fight you." Then he turned and walked away, leaving the rest flabbergasted.

I got fed up watching my Sunday school class doze off as I lectured. So on the bus to church one day, I took my notes and turned them into a series of questions. I shifted from telling to asking, with stunning success, and I adapted it for the rest of the year.

Eventually I was able to turn the teaching over to the kids. I remember one Sunday night, when Dorel was taking her turn to lead, the entire Jester gang showed up. Dorel was dealing with sexuality, and the gang members were disrupting the discussion with their giggling. Dorel could tell, by the glances they cast, who the gang leader was. So she told him that they had to all come in or leave. Not to be one-upped, the leader ordered all his guys to come in and shut up. It became quite a good discussion. When the evening was over, the gang leader pulled me aside and said that he was being sent to reform school. He was afraid what might happen to his boys in his absence. Would I be willing to take them over?

Sadly, I came down with mononucleosis and had to return to Texas to recuperate. But it was not in vain, and these apparent "nonentities" became remarkable human beings. Eddie earned his PhD in physics, Miriam entered a master's program in Hunter College, and Manny became a painter and nature photographer. And ah, Willy, you were a banker and you wanted to enter Hispanic politics, but you were murdered in a mugging.

After my first year in New York I was ready to get back to nature. So I wrote to Departments of Forestry all over the West. Only one bit: the state of Nevada, which operated two lookouts, one overlooking lovely Lake Tahoe and the other barren but beautiful. My then wife, Virginia, chose the latter, which went by the name "Peavine." There, I entered the Atomic Age.

The United States was still testing atomic bombs in the atmosphere at its nuclear site in Nevada. High levels of strontium 90 were reported in mothers' milk, and Virginia had become pregnant with our first son, Steve. I had even written Admiral Lewis Strauss, the head of the Atomic Energy Commission, about my concerns. He wrote back, reassuring me that states downwind from the testing were in much greater jeopardy and not to worry. For me, though, the issue of nuclear fallout became existential. And the testing went roaring on. One day, the radio announcer told us that the largest bomb ever exploded above American soil would be detonated that night. "Shasta" was its name. We went to bed with no further thought about it, when suddenly the entire lookout became incandescent. We were awestruck. We sat up in bed; then, as quickly as it came, it departed. When I returned to New York, I scouted out a lone bumper sticker to put on my dormitory door, and joined a lonely group with whom I could begin to resist the greatest terror humanity has ever let loose.

Peavine had lessons to teach me, though. At the lookout, I was supposed to check the horizon every fifteen minutes, but one afternoon when I was itching for exercise, I thought I could get back in time for the check. So I set out. When I got back to the station the radio was screaming, *"Peavine, Peavine, where are you, Peavine?"* I raced for the receiver and asked what was happening. *"Peavine, your mountain is on fire!"* Their concern was evacuating me if the fire took off. Fortunately they got control of the base of the mountain and I survived to watch another day. But imagine my embarrassment at failing to guard my own mountain! How apt an image for the necessity of introspection.

In the worldview of the new physics, everything is related. All the matter in the universe derives from the Big Bang (or better, the "Big Breath"). We are all one matter. Our bodies are virtually all water, and every drop of water in our bodies has been in every spring, every river, every lake, and every ocean during the last four and a half billion years on earth. We are all one water, observes Mary Coelho. Each breath we breathe contains a quadrillion (10^{15}) atoms, writes Guy Murchie, and more than a million of these atoms have been breathed personally sometime by each and every person on earth. We are all one breath. But we also breathe the dust of all those beings—people and pachyderms and plants—who have been vaporized in our warfare, our death camps, and our gulags. We are all one body, for good or ill. Likewise, attraction is characteristic of everything, from gravity to love. We are all one embrace. If ever a creature should feel at home in our universe, it is human beings.

That we are related to everything is no longer a hypothesis. Irish physicist John Stewart Bell posited the following theorem: "A change in the spin of one particle in a two-particle system will affect its twin simultaneously, even if the two have been widely separated." Put more simply, when oppositely paired particles are sent in opposite directions at the speed of light, even to the limits of the universe, and the spin of one is changed, the other particle's spin also changes, simultaneously. Eminent American physicist Henry Stapp has called this, with perhaps excessive praise, the most profound discovery in all of science.

In 1964, Bell had no idea whether his theorem was correct or not. But in 1972, John Clauser, a physicist at the University of California, Berkeley, was able to fashion an experiment that proved Bell right. Now Bell's theorem was a fact of the universe. But how could such a thing be possible? How did the second particle know that its partner's spin had changed? How could a message be transmitted from one to the other, since that would require speeds far exceeding the speed of light? And to suggest that anything could exceed the speed of light would be to cancel the very foundations of relativity theory, which seemed inconceivable. Finally it dawned on me: there is no distance. There is no distance for a message to traverse. Everything is already related. This means that the universe is a single, multiform energy-event characterized by nonlocality. German physicist Max Planck had already grasped the implication, stating that each individual particle of the system exists simultaneously in every part of the system. Hence, no particle can be explained, *except in reference to the entire cosmos.*

Once, after a lecture in Annapolis, Maryland, in which I made some uncomplimentary comments about scientists being caught up in the materialistic worldview, seven or eight physicists descended on me. "You don't know what you're talking about," they assured me. "We physicists talk about God more than any other department, including the religion department!" The new physics has opened a whole new way of perceiving, and relating to, reality. It will be decades before we take the measure of its accomplishment.

Mystics have long known this deeper dimension of reality. It is what John's Gospel called "eternal life" (John 17:3), or what Jesus called "the Kingdom of God in the midst of you" (Luke 17:21). Since everything is related, then, we have no need for actual physical contact in order to impact each other. Now that Bell's theorem has proven that there is no distance in nonlocal space, prayer and spiritual healing can now be understood as just the kinds of communication that we would expect from a world in which there is no distance.

The new physics made it possible for me to pray again. If there is no distance, then our prayers can be as effective halfway around the world as they can be in the hospital room, since nonlocal influence doesn't diminish with distance. Unlike local events, nonlocal interactions link up one location with another without crossing space, without decay, and without delay. If prayer doesn't have to go anywhere, then it may simultaneously be present everywhere, enveloping the praying party, the party prayed for, and the total field of reality, which we might call God. Instead of being a superstitious throwback to an irrational past, prayer can be seen as the highest kind of rationality.

THE PROBLEM OF OBJECTIVISM

At Union Theological Seminary, fellow student Steve Chinlund introduced me to the works of little-known Russian philosopher Nicolas Berdyaev, whose translated works I devoured. Steve had done an honors paper at Harvard in which he researched a war that had been described by three different observers, each claiming to have the "truth." Unacknowledged interests drove all three accounts. This means that there is no objective viewpoint that can be achieved by merging them into a single narrative. Pursuit of the problem of objectivism, which Steve flagged for me, became a sub-aspect in much of what I've written.

THE PARISH AND THE PHD

During my senior year at Union Theological Seminary, my favorite teacher, J. Christiaan Beker, called me into his office and asked me what I planned to do next. I said, "Become a parish minister in Texas." With his thick Dutch accent he said, "Vink, if you go into the parish the vay you are right now, you'll just be another loudmouthed Texan." It turns out that he had nominated me for a Rockefeller grant that would pay 100 percent of the cost of a PhD in New Testament. But it was restricted to scholars who planned to teach. In a burst of moralism I turned down the offer—and spent the rest of my life teaching!

AN EYE FOR AN EYE:
TURNING THE RIGHT CHEEK

Like the ancient myths in which a tiny creature, say a mouse, gnawed the rope that freed a lion, or like the Watergate complex, where a black janitor noticed the tape on the door latch, which led to the conviction of President Richard Nixon's advisors and his ultimate resignation, so too, I found that a single word led to the recovery of the true meaning of Jesus's saying on nonviolence. That word was "right."

I had been struggling with the passage in Matthew 5:39–41 that runs, "You have heard that it was said, '*An eye for an eye and a tooth for a tooth.*' But I say to you, do not resist an evildoer. But if anyone strikes you on the *right* cheek, turn the other also." That little word, "right," where did it come from? I had never noticed it before. Since adopting the Socratic method of teaching back during my field work in Harlem, I naturally asked the class I was teaching at the time what that little word, "right," was doing there. Nobody had a clue, the teacher included. It *was* the clue! In a moment of inspiration I suggested that a couple of people get up and role-play the text. Two volunteered. "Now," I began, "face off. Which of you will be the hitter, which the 'hittee'?" That settled, I said to the hitter, "How will you strike your opponent?" He made a fist and faked a blow with his right hand. But someone objected: the text doesn't say right *fist,* but right *cheek.* To strike the right cheek with the fist would require using the left hand, but in that society the left hand was used only for unclean tasks. Another student chimed in. The only way one could strike the right cheek would be with the *back of the right hand.*

I spent the weekend studying backhand blows, and brought my results to class. "What we are dealing with here is unmistakably an insult, not a fistfight. The intention is not to injure but to humiliate, to put someone in his or her 'place.'" I had learned that one normally did not strike a peer, and if he or she did the fine was exorbitant. A backhand slap, then, was the normal way of admonishing inferiors. Masters backhanded slaves; husbands, wives; parents, children; men, women; Romans, Jews. We have here a set of unequal relations, in each of which fighting back and retaliating would be suicidal. The only normal response would be cowering in submission.

This realization opened a floodgate for all sorts of new insights. It became important to ask who Jesus's audience is. Jesus's listeners are not those who strike, but their victims ("If anyone strikes *you*"). There were, among his followers, people who were subjected to these very indignities and forced to stifle their inner outrage. These were people who suffered dehumanizing treatment meted out to them by the hierarchical system of caste and class, race and gender, age and status, and as a result of imperial occupation. Why then does Jesus counsel these already humiliated people to turn the other cheek?

And it clicked: Because the action robs the oppressor of

the power to humiliate. The person who turns the other cheek is saying: "Try again. Your first blow failed to achieve its intended effect. I deny you the power to humiliate me. I am a human being just like you. Your status does not alter that fact. You cannot demean me."

Such a response would create enormous difficulties for the striker. Purely logistically, what can he do? He cannot use the backhand because the slave's nose is in the way. He cannot use his left hand regardless. If he hits with his fist, he makes himself an equal, acknowledging the other as a peer. The whole point of the back of the hand is to reinforce the caste system and its institutionalized inequality. Even if he orders the person flogged, the point has been irrevocably made. The oppressor has been forced, against his will, to regard this subordinate as an equal human being. The powerful person has been stripped of his power to dehumanize the other. This response, far from admonishing passivity and cowardice, is an act of defiance. How far this is from the passive reaction taught by the churches!

THE PROJECTS

I had not even thought of doing postgraduate studies, but I leaped at the idea. Without the Rockefeller grant I'd turned down earlier, I had little in the way of funds. Right then, the New York City Housing Authority approached Union Theological Seminary with a proposition: that Union would encourage a few students to move into Grant Houses, the project nearest to Union.

And so it happened that my friends Chuck and Patty Anderson and my small family integrated Grant Houses in reverse. We got to know the neighbor above us, who was a sky captain at LaGuardia Airport. He had been watching us, he said, figuring us to be communists because we were not only talking integration but acting it out. It didn't even occur to him that we might be Christians!

FULTON COUNTY, GEORGIA

In 1959, when Rev. Martin Luther King, Jr., was jailed in Fulton County, Georgia, my Union classmate John Stapleton and I organized a group of southern seminarians at northern seminaries to go there to witness against Rev. King's incarceration. There was some anxiety among us for fear of recriminations; the farther south, the greater the threat. But we managed to get two cars full, even in the dead of winter, even with no heater.

We demonstrated outside the jail and waved to Rev. King as he was moved to a different jail. We then had an interview with Atlanta mayor William Hartsfield, who gave us an off-the-record interview. Then we had a great conversation with Rev. Martin Luther King, Sr. at the Ebenezer Baptist Church, and then high-tailed it for home. The support of the Union community was terrific. But that was the whole point: southern seminarians in the North could act with relative impunity. Nevertheless, John's action was flashed all over South Carolina on TV and newspapers, so that he was barred from preaching in his home pulpit for a while. He was later formally vindicated by the United Methodist Church.

In New York, our five-year-old son Steve played with Jimmy, the black kid next door. But the following year, after moving back to Texas, my six-year-old son Steve gets the credit for integrating our Sunday school. He played with a black child while I talked to his mother about integrating the black and white churches. I can remember Steve coming home for lunch one day with a puzzled look on his face. *Daddy, what's a nigger?* He had to be taught.

. . .

When the black marchers crossed the Edmund Pettus Bridge in Selma, Alabama, in 1965 without a parade permit, they forced the authorities to decide between two courses. Either would damage their position: they could allow the blacks to march, thus recognizing the constitutional legitimacy of their protest, or the segregationists could forcibly stop it, thus exposing their own legal violence. The choice of violence was catastrophic for white supremacists and proved to be the turning point in the Civil Rights Movement. But the cost was terrible. As the marchers began to cross the bridge, white law enforcement personnel charged the protestors with clubs, tear gas, and attack dogs. The whole world watched, horrified.

Afterward, at the summons of Rev. Martin Luther King, Jr., clergy by the thousands descended on Selma. Ferd Dawson III, a young Texas preacher a few years my junior, and I drove from southeast Texas to join them. We were lent a credit card that we used a few times for gasoline on our trip that took us from southeast Texas, through Louisiana and Mississippi, to Alabama, the birthplace of the Confederacy. Our white polyester shirts virtually shouted "Nigger lovers," as we traversed the deepest southern states. By the time we drove into Alabama we noticed other cars from other states also arriving. It was a thrill to see that so many pastors, ministers, priests, rabbis, and concerned laity were descending on Selma. Still, Ferd and I were worried because we had heard reports on the radio that demonstrators were being severely beaten. In fact a Boston minister, Rev. James Reeb, had been beaten and on March 11 had died from his wounds. To demonstrate for civil rights came with a cost, and both Ferd and I knew this.

When we reached the outskirts of Selma, a pickup truck pulled up alongside us and the driver began cursing at us. He had a highly visible gun rack. Carefully I drove around looking for the church where the volunteers were assembling, but in vain. The driver of the pickup was now honking his horn. I was desperate. On the outskirts of town we had noticed a motel that had been completely taken over by the Alabama State Troopers. We didn't know what else to do but to go back there and throw ourselves on their mercy, a quality for which they were not exactly famous. We drove into the middle of their parked cars and saw another entrance that we might use as an exit. I can still feel how badly my legs were shaking as we drove away. I could scarcely keep them on the accelerator. In town, we asked a black teenager where the church was. He jumped in the car and took us there.

The next day we received mandatory training in nonviolence. The craven coward I felt like the day before had been transformed in three hours. I wish I could repeat what the trainers said, because three hours later we were ready to die for the cause of racial justice. Some nights later, a large crowd of black and white activists stood outside the Ebenezer Baptist Church, singing to pass the time. Suddenly a funeral home operator from Montgomery stormed the microphone. He reported that a group of black students demonstrating near the capitol just that afternoon had been surrounded by police on horseback. All had escaped, cynically commanded to disperse or take the consequences. Then the mounted police waded into the group of students and beat them at will. Police prevented ambulances from reaching the injured for two hours. Our informant was the driver of one of those ambulances, and afterward he had driven straight to Selma to tell us about it.

The crowd outside the church seethed with rage. Cries went up: "Let's march!" Behind us, across the street, stood, rank on rank, the Alabama State Troopers and the local police forces of Sheriff Jim Clark, itching for a fight. The situation was explosive. A young black minister stepped to the microphone and said, "It's time we sang a song." He opened with the line, "Do you love Martin King?" "Certainly, Lord!" the crowd responded. "Do you love Martin King?" "Certainly, Lord!" "Do you love Martin King?" "Certainly, certainly, certainly, Lord!" Right through the chain of command of the Southern Christian Leadership Conference he went, the crowd each time echoing, warming to the song, "Certainly, certainly, certainly, Lord!" Without warning he sang out, "Do you love Jim Clark?" "The sheriff?!" "Cer-certainly, Lord," came the stunned, halting reply. "Do you love Jim Clark?" "Certainly, Lord." It was stronger this time. "Do you love Jim Clark?" Now the point had sunk in: "Certainly, certainly, certainly, Lord."

The Reverend James Bevel then took the mike. We are not just fighting for our rights, he explained, but for the good of the whole society. "It's not enough to defeat Jim Clark—do you hear me, Jim?—we want you converted. We cannot win by hating our oppressors. We have to love them into changing."

. . .

Rev. King enabled his followers to see the white racist also as a victim of the Powers That Be, in this case the whole ethos of the southern way of life. Southern racists also needed to be changed. This provided a space and grace for transformation. While much more remains to be done in America than most of us like to think, change has occurred, datable to events like these, when the momentum of racist fury was stemmed by the willingness of a few people to absorb its impact with their own bodies and to allow it to spread no farther.

The real test came when we got home. Our small town in Texas was in an uproar, split over Ferd and me having gone to Selma. It was an unexpected referendum on the entire race issue, suddenly made concrete. My greatest gratification was the way our church members came to our defense. I decided to take the offensive. Every time I got wind of people who were badmouthing me, I would appear at their homes, no matter what church they belonged to, and sometimes harangue them for as much as two hours. It was exhausting. But Rev. King and Company had broken the moral backbone of Jim Crow, and no one had the courage to take me on. It took two months. Finally the backbiters were silenced. And this was happening all over the United States: the moral climate had changed, clergy were radicalized, and congregations awakened to the sin of racism.

PRAYER FOR GRACE

God, Lord and Judge and Forgiver, I affirm this day my commitment to you. I want to love you, care about you, nurture your life and power within me, rise from the death of my spirit. I can only offer myself, surrendered, to that which is greater and wiser than me. I want to be true to my own reality. Let me rest my weary soul in thee, Lord. Heal me, forgive me. Little Wind, spirit guide and guardian angel, I need further to believe in your help. I need to see that Jesus too depended on your help. O God, give me wisdom. Shield me from the side of me that might take over and destroy. Let me find the blessings here, though, where danger grows, the saving powers do as well.

After I received my doctorate from Union Theological Seminary, I was assigned to a little parish forty miles from Houston. I had always wanted to do parish work, and this blue-collar town was my chance. I went in as a green young pastor—right into the Civil Rights Movement!

We weren't a "liberal" church so much as an "open" church. If we could find warrants in the Spirit for needed change, we changed. We studied the Bible relentlessly. Every Sunday night we discussed the morning's sermon and its text. A definitive core of leadership emerged. There was plenty of conflict, but curiously, contention was usually not over civil rights or the escalating war in Vietnam, but power struggles in the leadership—the familiar lay leader and pastor struggle, which finally resolved itself after several years.

We integrated the schools, built a sanctuary, held healing services, and scandalized the district superintendent by introducing liturgical dance. And Sunday after Sunday I rediscovered how little help the publications being churned out by scholars were. I swore that I would find some way to redress this grievance if it took my whole life. It did.

Having had such wonderful success with "turn the other cheek," I wondered if the Bible offered additional clues to Jesus's teaching about nonviolence. The answer was almost instantaneous. Matthew 5:40 reads, "If anyone wants to sue you and take your coat, give your cloak as well." A student wondered out loud how people dressed in first-century Palestine. That was easily found: a long outer coat and a short inner jacket. Nothing else. Nothing else! Do you mean *naked*? The class burst into uproarious laughter. When they calmed down we reconstructed the situation: a creditor is hauling a debtor into court to get his long coat as collateral for an unpaid loan. Deuteronomy 24:10–13, 17 allows the court to seize the coat, but it must be returned by nightfall so that the poor man has something to sleep in. But it must be surrendered again in the morning.

Indebtedness was the most serious social problem in first-century Palestine. It is in this context that Jesus speaks. His hearers are the poor ("if anyone would sue *you*"). They share a rankling hatred for a system that subjects them to humiliation by stripping them of their lands, their goods, and finally even their outer garments. So why then does Jesus counsel them to give over their inner garment as well? This would mean stripping off all their clothing and marching out of court stark naked! Put yourself in the debtor's place, and imagine the chuckles this saying must have evoked.

We had such good luck with role-playing the earlier passage, I invoked the students to try it again. Now I must confess that I had set this scene up with one male student wearing a swimming suit under his clothes. He had agreed in advance to be the debtor. Then I picked a woman to be the creditor. Everything is improvisation. I played the judge. "Order in the court. What are the charges?"

> WOMAN: He owes me 50 denarii and he won't pay it back.
> JUDGE: How long?
> CREDITOR: Two years.
> JUDGE: Why haven't you paid her back?
> DEBTOR: My crops have failed, and my wife has been sick and I have ten children to feed.
> JUDGE: You know the law. If you won't repay her, you will have to give up your cloak.
> DEBTOR: Ah, Judge, it's cold out there. I'll freeze.
> JUDGE: You should have thought about that before you took out the loan. So give her your outer garment.

In our skit, the debtor reluctantly hands over the cloak. Then, while the Judge and Creditor make small talk, the Debtor goes through a transformation and bursts out:

DEBTOR: Well, look, if you're gonna take my cloak,
you might as well have my sandals, and my
socks. So you might as well take everything
I've got!

And with a flourish he drops his pants, revealing his
swimming suit. Pandemonium! I yell "Cut!" A most ani-
mated discussion ensues. Over the weeks that followed we
began to put words to the experience.

Put yourself in the debtor's place and imagine the guf-
faws this saying must have evoked. There stands the creditor, beet-red with embarrassment, your outer garment in
one hand and your underwear in the other. You have suddenly turned the tables on him. You had no hope of winning the trial; the law was entirely in his favor. But you have
refused to be humiliated, and at the same time you have
registered a stunning protest against a system that spawns
such debt. The creditor is revealed not to be a "respectable"
moneylender but to be a party in the reduction of an entire
social class to landlessness and destitution.

This unmasking is not simply punitive, however; it offers the creditor a chance to see, perhaps for the first time
in his life, what his practices cause, and to repent. Far from
collaborating in injustice, the poor man has used the law
to make an exploitative law a laughingstock. This message,
far from being a counsel of perfection unattainable in this
life, is a practical, strategic measure for empowering the
oppressed. It provides a hint of how to take on the entire
system in a way that unmasks its essential cruelty and to

burlesque its pretensions to justice, law, and order. Here is a poor man who will no longer be treated as a sponge to be squeezed dry by the rich. He accepts the laws as they stand, pushes them to the point of absurdity, and reveals them for what they really are. He strips nude, walks out before his compatriots, and leaves the creditor and the whole economic edifice he represents stark naked. Gandhi and King understood Jesus's aggressive, proactive nonviolence, but the churches on the whole embraced the so-called just war.

By now our class had begun to anticipate Jesus's sense of hilarity, so we were ready for the next one: "If anyone forces you to go one mile, go also the second mile." Roman soldiers had the right to force civilians to carry their packs for one mile, but one mile only. To force the civilian to go farther carried with it severe penalties under military law. In this way, Rome attempted to limit the anger of the occupied people and still keep its armies on the move. Nevertheless, this levy was a bitter reminder to the Jews that they were a subject people, even in the Promised Land.

But why walk the second mile? The question here is how the oppressed can assert their human dignity in a situation that cannot for the time be changed. The rules are Caesar's, but not how one responds to the rules—that is God's, and Caesar has no power over that. Imagine the soldier's surprise when, at the next mile marker, he reluctantly reaches to assume his pack (sixty-five to eighty-five pounds in full gear), and you say, "Oh, no, let me carry it another mile." Why would you do that? What are you up to? Normally he has to coerce your kinsmen to carry his pack, and now you do it cheerfully *and will not stop!* Is this a provocation? Are you insulting his strength? Being kind? Trying to get him disciplined for seeming to make you go farther than you should? Create trouble?

From a situation of servile impressments, you have once more seized the initiative. You have taken back the power of choice. The soldier is thrown off balance, having never dealt with such a problem before. Now, you have forced him into making a decision for which nothing has prepared him. If he has enjoyed feeling superior to the vanquished, he will not enjoy it today. Imagine the hilarious situation of a Roman infantryman pleading with a Jew, "Come on, please give me back my pack!" The humor of this scene may escape those who picture it with sanctimonious eyes, but it could scarcely have been lost on Jesus's hearers, who must have been delighted at the prospect of humiliating their oppressors.

Even if nonviolent action does not immediately change the heart of the oppressor, it does affect those committed to it. As Rev. Martin Luther King, Jr., attested, it gives oppressed people a new self-respect, calling up resources of strength and courage they did not know they had. To those who have power, Jesus's advice to the powerless may seem paltry. But to those whose lifelong pattern has been to cringe, bow, and scrape before their masters, and who have internalized their role as inferiors, this small step is momentous.

BACK TO UNION

After five very educative years in the parish in Texas, I returned to teach at Union Theological Seminary. These were the years, 1967–68, of the student revolution, the black economic development crisis, and the Black Panther Party bail fund, all of which brought Union into incredibly exciting and vitriolic turmoil. Resistance to the war in Vietnam resulted in a night in the Washington, DC, jail, a handful of arrests, and endless demonstrations. New forms of governance were sought that were more democratic and participatory. It was a time of heightened consciousness about racism, patriarchalism, and gay rights.

Through all of this I was attempting, with only small success, to relate the Bible to the upheaval we were undergoing. It had become clear to me in the parish that most biblical scholarship was irrelevant to the lived concerns of everyday people. The vast majority of scholars were now interested only in answering questions they each were asking. The community of accountability among biblical scholars had ceased to be the church and had become the academic guild of professional scholars. Now, back in an academy under siege, I sensed all the more powerfully the impotence of the detached, objective approach to Scripture for dealing with the real issues of life.

Dr. Warren Berland, another spiritual guide who had been so helpful to me, asked me to tell him about the religious experience that I had in Oregon. I had alluded to it several times, so I told him everything I was ashamed of. He was blown away. When I finished, he asked where I was now. I said I'd lost it. He said, "No, you can't lose it. You know this is the truth. Truth doesn't change. You may not feel it, but it is still the truth. You have experienced reality. You can never forget it. Have you told many people this story?"

"No, not many, not often," I replied. "I told a few class-mates, but they thought I had gone crazy, so I clammed up."

"Do you tell your students?"

"No."

"Why not?"

"Because I decided to honor the experience by help-ing them find their own experience of God. Gradually, though, I lost the immediacy of what had happened. Per-haps this came of having published most of my lectures. In an effort to simply do a good job, I have replaced the long-ing for the Holy Spirit. I do fewer experimental workshops than I'd like."

A long silence ensued. Finally Warren said:

"Faith means living the experience when it is not visible.

Your experience gave you an indomitable sense of life. Did God change God's mind? Do you think God no longer has any use for you? Don't you think God wants you healed? You know the truth. You cannot unknow it.

"God needs you, God wants you. Why do you think God doesn't? Because your ego gets in the way. Your ego won't let you get in touch with your essence. But that essence can't be taken away from you. Your essence is in you right now. Why do you let your ego rob you of the most wonderful experience you have ever had? It's amazing that you could turn your back on God! Your happiness is important to the whole world, especially to God. This is not an egoistic statement. The whole world is in thrall to our puny little egos, and we are destroying it at a horrendous rate. This collective egotism is what the Bible calls Satan. Didn't you write something about that?"

I felt as if I had been sprung from prison, as if I had been redeemed by a truth so plain that I was astonished that I had missed it.

Shortly thereafter I was walking across Central Park South, feeling very much caught "in the box," as Warren helpfully puts it. I was feeling alienated from everything, when suddenly I remembered that all I needed to do was step "out of the box" and into the world of God. I said to myself, "God is really real." Instantly I found myself in a different world.

The trees, so beautifully pruned, so majestic and prodigious, the fall flowers so lush and lovely, all said "God." As did a Bolivian ensemble playing in the park in front of the Plaza Hotel. And, as did an elderly black woman with a walker bracing herself by holding the spikes of the steel fence. I looked at her, made eye contact, and nodded. She nodded back, with a whispered acknowledgment. This was a sacred epiphany. Her pain, too, said "God."

Elizabeth Boyden Howes was a Jungian analyst and the founder of the Guild for Psychological Studies in San Francisco. It was from her that I learned something about the son of the man. She showed me how historical research depends on analogy to understand the past. If we have limited analogues—if for some reason our life experience is truncated, or too narrow, or filled with anxiety about overstepping the permissible—then our capacity to understand the past will suffer as a result. I was not able to enter empathetically into the spontaneity and boundary-shattering milieu of the early church, having been raised in a rationalistic, scholastic religion. I was circumscribed by deadly fears of heresy and dogmatically confined to an oppressive orthodoxy.

As I explored Jungian analysis, I began to sense that I had to do something about the poverty of my own self. Otherwise, I would be unable to proceed closer to the mystery in Scripture, but would simply continue to circle its perimeter, accumulating ever more information without myself being changed by the encounter. I began to understand that no scholar can construct a picture of Jesus beyond the level of spiritual awareness that he or she has attained. No reconstruction outstrips its reconstructor. We cannot explain truths we have not yet understood. We cannot present insights that we have not yet fathomed. Our picture of Jesus reflects not only Jesus, but the person portraying Jesus, and if we are spiritual infants or adolescents, there are whole realms of human reality that will simply escape us. In Revelation 1:19, the seer John is ordered, "Now write what you see." The problem lies precisely there, in sight: we can only describe what we see, and if we haven't seen it, we may miss the revelation entirely. It is my spiritual blindness that is the greatest impediment to my scholarship.

My integral worldview has emerged from a number of streams of thought: the new physics; the reflections of Sigmund Freud and Carl Jung on the unconscious; the ecstatic vision of paleontologist and priest Teilhard de Chardin; Rachel Carson and the environmental movement; the thought of process philosophers Alfred North Whitehead, Charles Hartshorne, John B. Cobb, Jr., and David Ray Griffin; Paul Tillich's "ground of being"; Thomas Merton; feminist theologians such as Beverly Harrison and Rosemary Radford Ruether; the writings of scientists Brian Swimme, Ian Barbour, John Polkinghorne, Arthur Peacocke, Gary Schwartz, and Fritjof Capra; Black religion; Celtic spirituality; the writings of theologians Morton Kelsey, Thomas Berry, and Matthew Fox; the engaged Buddhism of Thich Nhat Hanh and Joanna Macy; many Native American religions; and mystics, poets, and artists of every period and persuasion. From them, I have learned to see the outer and an inner aspect of everything.

Every institution, like every individual, has an outer physical reality and an inner spirituality. In Revelation 1 to 3, for example, "angels" are the spirituality, the ethos, or the corporate personality of a church. Those of us who have gone from church to church recognize how different the spirituality of different congregations is. Sometimes you enter and immediately sense something terribly pathological; at other churches, you feel a palpable impression of warm love and acceptance. And this is true of every corporate entity: they all have a corporate culture, spirit, or personality at the core of their reality. This spirit does not exist apart from its physical manifestations: its building, personnel, trucks, computers, territory, demographics, and so on. It is the *unity* of outer and inner that characterizes our experience of the integral worldview.

In the integral worldview, heaven and earth are seen as two dimensions of a single reality and affirms spirit at the core of every created thing. But this inner spiritual reality is inextricably related to an outer form or physical manifestation. It takes into account all the aspects of the traditional worldviews with which we began, but combines them in a different way. Both spiritual and materialistic worldviews use spatial imagery. The idea that heaven is "up" is a natural, almost unavoidable way of indicating transcendence. But that's all it is, a metaphor. For if the world turns, there is no longer an "up" anywhere in the universe, just as north is no more "up" than south is "down" on a map.

In the integral worldview, God's role in creation is literally true. God really is the creator, and science is the means of discovering how God did it. This is not creationism, which is simply a literalistic throwback to the traditional worldview. Rather, the integral worldview insists that if God is real, then God will have to be included in our theories of the nature of things. This holistic way of perceiving reality regards the new story of creation as *approximately true in a metaphoric sense.* Did God create the world? Definitely, though we are still trying to figure out how.

In the integral worldview, however, the soul permeates the universe. God is not just within us, but within everything. The universe is suffused with the divine. This is not pantheism, where everything is God, but panentheism (*pan,* everything; *en,* in; *theos,* God), where everything is in God and God is in everything. Spirit is at the heart of everything, even down to the smallest particle of spirit-matter. Hence all creations are potential revealers of God. This integral worldview is no more essentially "religious" than the traditional worldview, but I believe it makes the biblical data more intelligible for people today than any other available worldview, including the traditional one.

Yet the materialists would have us believe that we are alien to what is. Quite the contrary, everything *interpenetrates* everything else. Sperm and ovum unite, becoming related. We are already related to our mother in her womb. We enter life with relationships of every kind. Babies cannot even survive without human touch. We are not isolated billiard balls knocking up against each other as if we were essentially separate and alone. Rather, we are a hive of seven billion humans, always already related in myriad forms. We must be taught to be alienated, to hate, to kill. This to me is the profound sadness and waste of the existentialists, with their painful angst at having to create meaning in a meaningless universe. In his play *No Exit,* Jean-Paul Sartre said, "Hell is—other people." But try living without them. Other people are hell only when they are deprived of genuine relatedness, attraction, and love.

However, it might be instructive to contrast the role of prayer in the supernaturalistic worldview with the integral worldview. In the former, one might pray for spiritual healing. But because the supernaturalistic worldview allows no real contact between the realm of science and that of theology, or between body and spirit, spiritual healing and prayer would be inappropriate, even foolish. And so another slick adage is born: God may not cure us (physically), but God can heal us (spiritually). That adage is no doubt true in some cases, but it can also be a cop-out when it is used as a way to avoid prayer for actual physical healing.

In the integral worldview, however, prayer is given the place of honor in the life of the spirit. Since we are all already related to each other, we are immediate to each other. So prayer becomes the most natural thing in the world. We don't have to pump ourselves up in order to release a charge of healing energy. The other persons don't even have to know we are praying for them. Because we are already related, and we are one body in God, God's healing power is already there and here (but there is no distance). Our prayer is simply a matter of opening the situation to God.

Over one hundred years ago, the Nobel Prize–winning scientist Alexis Carrel commented that in the future, scientists would take love into the laboratory and find more power there than in the atom. His prophecy is being enacted before our eyes. What an exciting challenge: to be able to help shape that new, integral worldview along lines that honor life, the environment, and the very universe itself. This is a view that sees the whole teeming world as a revelation of God.

I had experienced spiritual healing in Oregon at the Pentecostal Church. So when I became a pastor, I inaugurated a healing service. My ministerial colleagues that I shared this with thought I was crazy. The Friday before our first healing service I received a call from a member of our church, a woman who had just been told by her doctor that she had a tumor in her uterus the size of an orange. I cheerfully told her that that would be nothing for God to heal, and to show up Sunday night. Being of a literal cast of mind, she believed me. At the service we laid on hands and prayed, and the next week she went back to her doctor. "I have the biopsy report here on my desk," he said," "but first let's have a look at you." Then he asked, "Who's been messing with you!?" "Why?" she asked. "It's gone. Your tumor's gone!" He seemed somehow disappointed.

Because of that, and many similar experiences with spiritual healing, I have no difficulty believing that Jesus actually healed people, and not just of psychosomatic diseases. Other scholars, who have never experienced such healing, in either themselves or others, may find themselves rejecting the historicity of the healing stories as a totality. They might even defend their understanding of reality by deciding that the story I just told is untrue. This judgment, however, would be made not on historical grounds, but on the basis of their worldview, which is materialism. Historical discussion is often made to bear the weight of what are essentially differences of worldview, which cannot in principle be settled by historical method. Worldviews are constituted by what one believes about the nature of reality, and therefore by what one conceives to be possible—what Paul Ricoeur called "the available believable." These experiences enrich our sense of the possible.

In the first seminar I attended at the Guild for Psychological Studies in San Francisco, one of the early exercises was to take the story of the Healing of the Paralytic in Mark 2:1–12 and internalize it by making in clay my own inner paralytic. I had a PhD and a prestigious academic appointment; I "had" no paralytic. Life was careening along just fine, I thought. But to be a good sport I tried it. Shutting my eyes, as they suggested, I let my hands have their way. After a period of time had passed, I looked to see what my hands had done. They had made a beautiful bird—with a broken wing! I am no artist, and was simply astonished that my hands had done this. More significant still, I suddenly knew precisely what that broken-winged bird was in me: an atrophied-feeling function.

Thus began the task of recovering my capacity to feel, which was to last, in earnest, for the next eight years. I carried a notebook everywhere so I could jot down feelings I had during the course of the day. The harvest was few. Many days I had only one, or none. But I kept at it, fitfully. I immediately adapted what I was learning to my classes. The students loved it, but my colleagues were a bit put off by the notion of graduate students working in clay and pastels like Sunday school kids.

THE BUDDHIST NOVICE

There were few moments of insight during my restless nights, but one was inescapable. It came by way of a dream. In my journal, I wrote:

> I am trying to join a Buddhist order or some-thing like it. The Master comes in. There must be thirty in the group of prospective novices. Each of us, in turn, is to open the door. (It opens into the room.) The first was a Japanese guy. He spends only a few seconds on the task, then quits. The Master dismisses him with a few words. I am next. We have been given no instructions. I have no idea how much time we have. I have a pointed stick. I use it to lever the door. Unfortunately, I apply pressure on the hinge side, and I come up short. I stop. The Master gives a devastating critique. He doesn't comment on my attempt to open the door, but rather on me. "You are unsure of yourself," etc. (I can't recall his words.) He dis-misses me. I am devastated. I decide to quit if this kind of critique continues.
>
> Next we are to gather in a rectangular build-ing. It is several blocks away. I am carrying some-

thing on my shoulders. I have started too late, and he warned that anyone late will be locked out. I am late, but the door is still open. But it is such a long way, and I can't run because of the burden.

I have come to understand, with the aid of my helpers, that I am trying to find a way, but I have no idea how. But I don't give up, even though the Master has devastated me with his accurate critique. The burden is too much. I have two choices: let the burden hold me back, or keep on trying these different ways. The Master will be there even though I'm late.

The other prospective novice is a birthright Buddhist. He was born into a Buddhist milieu, and yet he has no advantage. There is a Buddhist Master in my soul whose task it is to open the door to my soul. I am taking on a new life's task, and the door is opening out toward me. There's a Buddhist Master who wants to help me open the door inside me. But both the Japanese guy, who went before me, and I went too fast. We should have stopped to meditate, and asked the door what it needs in order to open. Maybe I should have just grabbed the knob and barged in. (Though that smells suspiciously like the way I have been opening doors these seventy-two years.)

The Master has given us no help in figuring out how to open the door. He seems to be deliberately inducing failure so that we will realize that we don't know how to become novices. I think I am a spiritual person, but this reveals me as not even able to be a novice! I was ready to give up—I don't know how to be human, and instead of giving up trying, I am challenged to try to become a novice even though I have no idea how. The burden—restless leg syndrome?—is keeping me from getting there on time. I fail again, but the door has been left open anyway.

I'm a novice who isn't even a novice. The novice moves ahead by acknowledging that he or she doesn't know how to do the task. The Dream-Master is prepared for the next phase of my life. The task as a novice is to know that he or she doesn't know. A beginner's mind is necessary. My deep unconscious is aware that I'm in the process of ending this phase of my life. What has made me successful in an earlier phase will not be helpful in the next. I'm coming to the time of entering the eternal. But there is a new world opening. I'm a field that needs to be planted. But first it must lie fallow. I need to know that I don't know and that there is a Master who does, and I must learn to trust him.

PRAYER FOR KNOWLEDGE
from 1975

Oh thou source, well up in me this day that you're anointing way be upon my classes, not so we may have a "good" experience, but so that each discovers you as source.

I must continue to hold out for language that states what is real to experience, and images that actually evoke the source rather than images that evoke the memory of the source.

Is it the radicalism of nonviolent resistance which yet submits to the authority of the state to punish? Can there be any other sense in Paul's own frequent trips to jail? And beating on the Roman rods? Contrast the radical peaceniks; it is not my government! Reject dissociation.

EZEKIEL'S VISION*

Ezekiel 1 is so overwhelming in its surplus of powerful symbolic images that the rabbis only permitted mature persons to read this chapter, and then only in the company of a person who was older and wiser. A saying, often repeated in Jewish lore, stated that four Jewish mystics succeeded in ascending to heaven and viewing the divine throne-chariot that Ezekiel describes. One went mad, one became a heretic, one died, and only Rabbi Akiba returned in his right mind. These popular warnings indicated profound respect for the raw psychic power of the spiritual world. These mystics recognized that these archetypal images and symbols were not just a manner of speaking, but that they were capable of transforming—or unhinging—those who encountered them.

The immediate political context for Ezekiel 1 is crucial to understanding the vision. It was 593 BCE. Ezekiel was by the River Chebar in Babylon in the fifth year of the exile of King Jehoiachin and the bulk of the Jewish aristocracy. Those remaining in Jerusalem, who had escaped exile,

* Previously published in Walter Wink, *The Human Being: Jesus and the Enigma of the Son of the Man* (Minneapolis, MN: Fortress Press, 2001).

persisted in believing that they had weathered the worst, and that the exile of their leaders had diverted the attention of the empire away from tiny Israel. But "tiny Israel" was located on the land bridge between the Middle East and Egypt. Israel thus was critical to the geopolitics of any empire of that region and period. Whoever controlled Palestine was poised to attack any of the major rivals to political control. Six years after this vision, in 587 BCE, Zedekiah, the new king of Judah, revolted against Babylon and brought about the destruction of Jerusalem, including the razing of the temple and the walls of the city. Israel had grown accustomed to localizing Yahweh in the Jerusalem Temple, however expansive the divine reach might be from there. But now Ezekiel was in exile, in a foreign land presided over by Marduk, the god of Babylon, who had, to judge by history, defeated Yahweh. It was a time of crisis for Israel. It fell to Ezekiel to reveal to his people that Yahweh was sovereign and could speak and intervene in a foreign land, even without the temple. Ezekiel's vision in exile comes, then, at one of the critical points in Jewish history, when the very survival of faith hung in the balance.

At the heart of Ezekiel's vision is this astonishing statement:

> And above the dome of their heads there was something like a throne, in appearance like sapphire; and seated above the likeness of the throne was something that seemed like a human form (Adam).
>
> Upward from what appeared like the loins I

saw something like gleaming amber, something that looked like fire enclosed all around; and downward from what looked like the loins I saw something that looked like fire, and there was a splendor all around.

Like the bow in a cloud on a rainy day, such was the appearance of the splendor all around. This was the appearance of the likeness of the glory of the Lord. When I saw it, I fell on my face, and I heard the voice of someone speaking (Ezek. 1:26–28).

He said to me: O mortal ("son of man"), stand up on your feet, and I will speak with you (Ezek. 2:1).

This is one of the most understated visionary reports ever recounted. Against all tendencies toward exaggeration, Ezekiel goes out of his way, redundantly, to stress that he is doing the best he can to describe the indescribable. Yet he knows that his words are not enough, that he cannot do the vision justice. His descriptions bend and break while the experience races ahead of language. A fictionalized account would have been full of certainty and precision; Ezekiel qualifies virtually every word of his report.

Now the vision breaks to the center, and the qualifications and hesitations stumble all over themselves: "And above the dome over their heads there was *something like* a throne, *in appearance like* sapphire; and seated above the *likeness* of a throne was *something* that *seemed like* a human form" (Ezek. 1:26).

And this is the revelation: God is HUMAN.

This is no anthropomorphism. Israel was thoroughly familiar with anthropomorphic language, and never confused it with reality. If you asked Jews if God was walking in the Garden of Eden in the cool of the day because the heat was disagreeable (Gen. 3:8), they would have dismissed the question as impertinent: Of course not, that is only a figure of speech.

But Ezekiel is not beholding a figure of speech. This is really what God is: HUMAN. It is the great error of humanity to believe that it is human. We are only fragmentarily human, fleetingly human, brokenly human. We see glimpses of our humanness, we can dream of what a more human existence and political order would be like, but we have not yet arrived at true humanness. Only God is human, and we are made in God's image and likeness—which is to say, we are capable of becoming human.

Furthermore, we are incapable of becoming human by ourselves. We scarcely know what humanness is. We have only the merest intuitions and general guidelines. Jesus has, to be sure, revealed to us what it means to live a fully human life. But how do I translate that into my own struggles for humanness? Curiously enough, I now know more about God, thanks to Jesus, than I do about myself. God is the ultimate mystery, yes, but to myself I am an even more impenetrable mystery. Who am I? I have accepted my parents' answers, my culture's answers, the answers of mentors and peers and colleagues. But how do they know? What are the exact outlines of my true form? What is the visage of my real face? How can I find out, unless God reveals it to me? For who else could possibly know what is stored up in the divine image inside me, except that one who is the divine image inside me?

So this is not Operation Bootstrap, trying to lift ourselves up into our own potential. We must, it is true, be constantly attentive to the clues being provided, oh so gradually, in prayer, in Scripture, in worship, in preaching, and in silence, dreams, and meditation—and, yes, also from our parents, our culture, our mentors, and our peers and colleagues, and perhaps, above all, from our enemies. As one of the most remarkable lines of Scripture puts it, "Beloved, we are God's children now; what we will be has not yet been revealed. What we do know is this: when he (or 'it') is revealed, we will be like him, for we will see him as he is" (1 John 3:2).

Karl Barth showed his grasp, in a more cautious but affirmative way, of the humanity of God. In his book, audaciously entitled *The Humanity of God,* he writes, "It is precisely God's *deity* which, rightly understood, includes [God's] *humanity.* . . . It is when we look at Jesus Christ that we know decisively that God's deity does not exclude but includes [God's] *humanity.* . . . God is *human* . . . genuine deity includes in itself genuine humanity. . . ."

This revelation comes to Ezekiel toward the beginning of the Babylonian captivity. At something about the same time, the creation story in Genesis 1 was being crafted as an answering rebuke to the Babylonian creation myth, the *Enuma Elish.* In the Babylonian myth, human beings are created from the blood of a murdered god in order to serve the gods. Genesis 1 asserts, to the contrary, that all creation is good, and that human beings are created in God's image:

> Then God said, "Let us make humankind in our image, according to our likeness; and let them have dominion. . . ." So God created human-kind in the divine image; in the image of God God created them; male and female God created them. (Gen. 1:26–27)

Bill Wylie-Kellermann comments,

> Human Beings are the image of God. Here is an idea so incredibly subversive it may be the most politically loaded claim of all. Who in Babylon, not to mention virtually the whole of the ancient world, was the image of God? The King, of course, who stands in for [Babylonian God] Marduk in the creation pageant, and whose authority is annually legitimated. Who, however, is in the liturgy of Israel? Humanity. Women and Men. Human Beings in community. This is a subversion and affront to every imperial authority. It's practically anarchism. In this counter-story human beings are not created from the blood from a murdered god, created as slaves of the state. They are made for freedom and responsibility.

And because humans are like God and God is like humans, the shedding of human blood is prohibited (Gen. 9:4–6; Ezek. 33:25). Our being in the image of God thus has ethical consequences. Gerhard von Rad suggests plausibly that Genesis 1 is directly prompted by the revelation God gave Ezekiel, and is the first elaboration of it. Scholars have long noted that Genesis 1 is too rational and abstract to really be a myth. It was a polemic made possible by the unprecedented breakthrough of Ezekiel's vision.

To be in the image of God is to be *of* the same stuff, the same essence, the same being, masculine and feminine. But we humans are clearly not "like" God in our mundane existence. We are selfish, contentious, brutal, indifferent, vicious, and vindictive. If we are like God, then, we are so only potentially. Perhaps someday we might become more fully human. For now, we are only promissory notes, hints, intimations.

If God is true humanness, then divinity inverts. Divinity is not a qualitatively different reality; quite the reverse, *divinity is fully realized humanity.* Only God is HUMAN. The goal of life, then, is not to become something we are not—divine—but to become what we truly are—human. We are not required to become divine: flawless, perfect, without blemish. We are invited simply to become human, which means growing through our sins and mistakes, learning by trial and error, being redeemed over and over from sin and compulsive behavior, becoming ourselves, scars and all. Is it not the case that the deepest reaches of our humanity are born of our wounds, even through our sins?

Eastern Orthodoxy has long taught that the goal of human existence is to become "divinized." I have deep respect for the spiritual disciplines that have been developed in order to further this process of growth into God. Somehow the Eastern churches have succeeded in hedging divinization about with a received wisdom that prevents inflation on the part of the mystical adept. But those of us who have been raised in the Western church traditions are fairly defenseless in the face of such grand aspirations, and our egos all too quickly identify with the deep Self at our core—the image of God—and go launching out into the stratosphere of delusional self-worship and narcissism.

Divinization is too dangerous for most of us in the West, and besides, I have no idea what it means. When people say Jesus is divine, or son of God, or God, I have nothing in my experience that can help me comprehend what is meant. It all sounds too much like the language of Greek polytheism, in which gods impregnated mortal women, who bore beings who were half human and half divine. The interminable debates about the two natures of Christ seem to me to be totally off the mark, an irrelevancy carried over from a worldview that is now virtually defunct for all but the truest of true believers. I do not mean to attack anyone's faith. I merely wish to indicate why I find the revelation that came to Ezekiel so appealing. I do not know what the word "divine" signifies. But I do have an inkling of what the word "human" might entail, because we are made in the image of God, and have seen Jesus.

Central to the Eastern Orthodox tradition is a statement by Athanasius of Alexandria that Christ became as we are that we might become as he is. This has usually been interpreted as meaning that Christ became human that we might become divine. I hear it saying rather that Jesus became like us—people living within the constraints of earthly reality—in order that we might become like him—fully human. But that way of speaking is still too traditional for me. I would prefer to say, Jesus incarnated God in his own person in order to show all of us how to incarnate God. And to incarnate God is what it means to be fully human.

But we risk losing the numinous reality under a barrage of words. Ezekiel is not struck as if by an interesting new idea. He is, rather, struck to the ground. The vision overwhelms him, like a blow to the solar plexus. And the God who has struck him now orders him to his feet. God, apparently, will not converse with human beings supinely prostrated. That which addresses us insists that we stand our ground. God will not speak as to an inferior, will not tolerate a servile mentality. The Spirit enters Ezekiel to embolden him to face this awesome vision.

The Human One on the throne-chariot now addresses Ezekiel: "Child of the Human One, stand up on your feet, and I will speak with you" (Ezek. 2:1). Chip off the old block, Humanchild in exile, this offspring of the HUMAN will from henceforth not be addressed by his given name, but only as a relative of the enthroned one. This name, *ben adam,* is the mysterious outcome of this mysterious encounter. In the moment that one faces the Glory of God, the Child of the Human is born. To see God as Human is to become what one sees. What is born is a person able to face and to carry this power. Ezekiel has received a name for what emerges when a person withstands God's glory without crumbling, fleeing, or becoming inflated. The Child of the Human is the *imago dei*, that within us that has been potential from the beginning but which had not come to conscious awareness and accessibility. By addressing the prophet as Humanchild, God indicates that humanizing humanity is the divine purpose. In this absolutely seminal vision, one of the most significant in human annals, God is shown moving toward human beings, toward manifestation, toward eventual incarnation and co-creative partnership.

Ezekiel needed some such overwhelming vision, for he is being sent as a prophet to a rebellious people who will not listen. What draws us to the sufferings of God's messengers is not perfection but broken wholeness. As my first New Testament teacher, J. Christiaan Beker, once said to me, with deliberate insinuation: "Our dreams of perfection are our greatest sins." It is in the crucifixion of our idealized self-images that we discover our true being, which includes those aspects that we would rather disown. This focus on perfectionism thus brings me full circle from the storeroom to the present.

> He said to me, Human Being [*ben adam*], I am sending you to the people of Israel, to a nation of rebels who have rebelled against me; they and their ancestors have transgressed against me to this very day. The descendants are impudent

and stubborn. I am sending you to them, and
you shall say to them, "Thus says the Lord God."
Whether they hear or refuse to hear (for they are
a rebellious house), they shall know that there
has been a prophet among them. (Ezek. 2:3–5)

Ezekiel's community of accountability and support has
shrunk to one—the Creator of the ends of the earth. This
vision sustains him in the face of the non-responsiveness
of his own people. God gives him an adamantine forehead,
like the hardest stone, harder than flint, to resist the stub-
bornness of his equally hardheaded people (Ezek. 3:8–9).
He is not God's ventriloquist-dummy, mouthing the words
God speaks through him. "Humanchild, eat this scroll,
and go, speak to the house of Israel" (Ezek. 3:1). Ezekiel is
to *digest* the word of God and articulate it in his own words
and tongue. He does not open his mouth and let the words
pour forth in a mantic trance state. Rather, he apparently
writes his prophecies, and then presents the carefully considered result to the people. God is not speaking *through*
the prophet, but speaking *to* the prophet, who then must
present as exactly as he is able God's word to a recalcitrant
people. Yet Ezekiel frequently closes a sentence or para-
graph with "I Yahweh have spoken (it)."

Ezekiel is thus the recipient, not the source, of the au-
thoritative word. And this, says Ellen Davis, served him
well in speaking an unwelcome word to rebellious Israel.
By portraying himself as a listener rather than an initia-
tor of speech, Ezekiel emphasizes the divine initiative in

the communication. Repeatedly we are reminded that Ezekiel is the unwilling vehicle, not the originator, of this message.*

As Humanchild, Ezekiel is thus a representative and intermediary between God and people. The Humanchild seems to be that aspect of Ezekiel capable of discerning and transmitting what the Human One intends for humanity. It is, as it were, prophetic receptivity, the capacity to enter into communication with God. "Humanchild" thus resonates strikingly with the Quaker expression, "that of God within us." The fragile, finite earth creature that is exalted with glory and honor in Psalm 8 is here charged with a mission from God to the "children of the Human" (*benei adam*, 31:14) who have lost their ears. The Humanchild is not, then, a spokesperson for the people, but for God; the Humanchild is merely a representative of the people.

Later Jewish commentators made much of the fact that what Ezekiel saw on the throne that day was not the divine totality, but only "the appearance of the likeness of the glory of the Lord" (Ezek. 1:28). God's Glory was regarded in later Judaism as a surrogate for God, a stand-in, merely a single aspect of a reality too powerful and complex for any human to endure. To see the divine totality would destroy a person. God therefore condescends to show, as it were, only that of God that we fragmentary humans can bear, comprehend, and assimilate. God is like the power in the high-voltage lines that originate at Niagara Falls. Touch

* Ellen F. Davis, *Swallowing the Scroll* (New York: Bloomsbury T&T Clark, 2009), 82–83.

them, and we fry. We need a transformer that can reduce the voltage to something usable. By calling the figure on the throne the Glory of God, the Jewish mystics were acknowledging that what they were experiencing was not God in all God's fullness, but God in a form that aspiring human beings can take in without being overwhelmed. What the mystics saw, following Ezekiel, was the human face of God—God as humanity needs to know God in order to become what God calls us to be. We become what we behold. So God offers us the gift of our own humanity, not as something to be attained, but as pure revelation. God is a mirror in which we find reflected our own "heavenly," that is, potential, face. As the late first-century *Odes of Solomon* 17:4 put it,

> *My chains were cut off by His hands;*
> *I received the face and likeness of a new person,*
> *And I walked in Him and was saved.*

In the vision, however, Ezekiel does not experience God as clear and distinct. The Human One on the throne is more like a silhouette engulfed by fire (Ezek. 1:27). The divine mystery of the humanness of God is not, then, fully disclosed to Ezekiel, but rather compounded into the final human mystery. Does this suggest that God is emergent with us? That God is also in process of becoming? That God is, reciprocally, wanting to take on human form, wanting to incarnate in us?

Ezekiel's reticence before the final mystery is remarkable. His repetitious insistence that he is only describing "the appearance of the likeness" of this reality reminds us that we lack the capacity to know what we are really talking about. Though I have attempted to understand this vision in all seriousness, I must warn the reader that everything I have said is only reflection twice removed, an approximation of an approximation.

ON TEACHING THE BIBLE

At Union Theological Seminary, I began searching for a better way to do biblical work, one that would place the relevance of the text for contemporary life, not at the end of the endeavor but include it from the outset. I began to explore the various technologies of the "human potential movement," finding much that was helpful to me personally and professionally in a general framework of narcissism and naïveté about the depth of human evil.

My goal in teaching was to free people from depending on experts, while using expert knowledge. I have striven to find a way that empowers my congregation and classrooms to find God's word in community, while enhancing the Bible's power to challenge what we believe God's word to be. I strive to combine educational form and educational content with integrity, to find a way to provide information along the path to fundamental personal and social transformation. In short, a way that is consistent with the Bible's own reason for being.

THE COLUMBIA UNIVERSITY BUST

The faculty of Union Theological Seminary believed that a younger teacher might have better rapport with the students. What they got instead was a younger faculty radical! When students seized Columbia University buildings, destroying the life's work of scholars, they forfeited widespread support. In an attempt to create "participatory democracy," Union was invited to join the strike steering committee. Professor Paul Lehmann and I were the only faculty members elected in the entire Columbia complex.

This required attendance at endlessly boring strategy meetings. At the same time, leaders were emerging who were demagogues intent on rising to the top. Mark Rudd was one of these. People were afraid to cross him or simply to disagree with him, myself included. I began to boycott the meetings. I yielded my place to a "new" Union student whom I had never seen before, very clean shaven, and who was surely a federal agent.

The Columbia Bust was successful in some of its demands—abandoning plans to build a gym in Morningside Park and the firing of the president, to name a few. But the violence in the Columbia Bust left permanent scars.

When I published *The Bible in Human Transformation* (Philadelphia: Fortress Press, 1973), with its infamous opening line, "Historical biblical criticism is bankrupt," my fellow biblical faculty greeted it politely, with demurrers, but largely simply waited for my tenure to come up. When it did, they voted it down. Since that book had also incensed large numbers of other biblical scholars elsewhere, I found myself young, virtually blacklisted—and unemployed. One fellow scholar, when I introduced myself, said, "Oh yes, I read your book; I disagree with everything you say." Another simply turned his back on me. Such behaviors (and there were others) opened old wounds of rejection. I stopped going to scholarly meetings for five years, until the reverberations of the storeroom rejection receded. But it took a lot of work.

CHILE

Without realizing it, I had turned a corner. My involvement in social action throughout the 1950s and '60s was episodic, but in the succeeding decades I became completely involved. In 1982, I wanted to really know what it was like to live under a dictatorship. With the help of Chilean missionaries I'd met, my present wife, June, and I found a place to live in a room with a shower in a Methodist church in Santiago. We had some pretty tough digs in New York City, but they were nothing like showering in the melted snow of the Andes. The toilet kept stopping up and overflowing. We had to "cook" with a little coil you would stick in your cup. But we fed off the streets: empanadas and the finest peaches we have ever eaten.

June had taught a Chilean child at Riverside Church nursery/kindergarten, and they were going home the same time we were going to visit. So when they heard our hilarious descriptions of our room, they insisted that we stay with them, which we did, for the better part of several months! It turns out that we had landed in a circle of poets, architects, philosophers, and painters. Our host, Virgilio, was one of Chile's finest poets; he was the center of it all, in a house bulging with books. Eventually, Virgilio found a cottage for us.

After observing Chilean culture and becoming close to those we met, I observed four possibilities for the Chilean resistance to their military dictatorship:

1. *Be passive and simply wait it out.* This is most feasible when there is hope of the collapse of the ruling power. This seems to have been the choice of the Chileans we met. It is a valid choice. But this option puts no pressure on those who remain, and one must be constantly on guard against cowardice.

2. *Violent resistance.* The Chilean military was so powerful that this kind of resistance is foolhardy. An attempt was made on Pinochet's life, but the wrong car was hit, and the very failure reinforced hopelessness.

3. *Nonviolent resistance.* This is the most hopeful alternative to the present order. It is not passive; resistance is encouraged. But the manner is nonviolent. For example: small coteries discover the houses where torture is happening. They also measure the distance from the police post to the torture house. On signal, they arrive at the torture house and take out signs that read "Torture Happens Here." When the time allotment is over, they pin the signs to the fence and disappear in all directions. Another tactic was so effective that it inaugurated the fall of Pinochet: a whisper campaign setting a date for opponents all over the country to bang on pots and pans,

and blow whistles and honk horns, expressing rejection of the Pinochet regime. At first people were timid, but when the noise became an uproar, and then bedlam, it became clear that the regime was no longer legitimate. People had no idea that the dissatisfaction ran so deep. In a matter of only months, the Pinochet regime was voted out of office.

4. *Voluntary exile.* This position also puts no pressure on the regime, but there are numerous reasons that some people must save their own lives on behalf of their people, especially if their own people consent.

The Vicariate of Solidarity of the Roman Catholic Church was the rallying point of resistance in Chile, and did what it could to document torture and disappearances from the very outset of the military takeover. It was striking how openly the people criticized the government. They seemed to push the margin of defiance to the very limit, just shy of arrest. It was deeply moving to see people struggling to be human in the very maw of oppression, and they were doing it.

PEACE FELLOW

My growing interest in nonviolence led to an appointment as a Peace Fellow for the years 1989–90 at the United States Institute of Peace in Washington, DC. From there, June and I led workshops on nonviolence in Jerusalem, Zimbabwe, Namibia, South Africa, Chile, Argentina, Trinidad and Tobago, East and West Germany, Canada, Mexico (nonviolence training for the Zapatista insurgency), England, Northern Ireland, Scotland, and, of course, our own United States. I also made a solo trip to lecture on nonviolence in South Korea.

My preoccupation most of these years had been to facilitate personal and social transformation through Scripture and art, movement and meditation. It was with genuine gratitude that June and I became joint recipients of the Fellowship of Reconciliation's annual Martin Luther King, Jr., Peace Award in 2006 "for our lifelong commitment to promote peace, justice, and reconciliation." We were selected "from among many others like yourselves whose life and work have enhanced the opportunities for a peaceful world." The award recognizes all "unheralded persons or groups working . . . in the tradition of Dr. King." Any number of other individuals were more worthy. I take it that we were eligible due to our anonymity, and that we were representative of them all.

ARGENTINA

June and I crossed the towering Andes Mountains from Chile to Argentina, only to land in the middle of the Malvinas/Falklands War. With real lives at stake, England and Argentina fought over possibly the most worthless scrap of real estate in the world. I asked the Protestant theological faculty in Buenos Aires if they thought it was a just war. They replied, "Yes, to a man." Eight years later, while visiting the University of Oxford, I put the same question to the British ethicists there, and they answered, "Yes, to a man." To my mind, the most judicious response was given by the Argentinean Nobel Peace Prize laureate, Adolfo Pérez Esquivel, who argued that the historical and geographical claim of Argentina was stronger, but that Argentina could have won the struggle by nonviolent means.

In 1976, Argentina suffered a military takeover when right-wing Argentine army commander Jorge Rafael Videla deposed Isabel de Martínez Perón to become de facto president. Videla and General Reynaldo Bignone then began a crusade to crush leftists as they rose to prominence. Both men were noted for human rights abuses, which drew public condemnation from President Jimmy Carter's administration for four years.

By the time we were visiting Argentina in 1982, President Ronald Reagan was in office and support for the Argentinean government strengthened. The Reagan administration turned a deaf ear when it was reported that women suspected of communist leanings had their babies taken from them by the government. In some reported cases, pregnant mothers were kept alive long enough to give birth. Backed by the United States and its School of the Americas, the Argentinean military trained its personnel in techniques for controlling the populace, including torture.

All opponents were branded "communist" and rounded up, and between nine thousand and thirty thousand were "disappeared" (the figure is imprecise because the military won the right to destroy all records). The preferred method of execution was drugging the victims and dropping them naked from thirteen thousand feet into the Atlantic Ocean. Catholic military chaplains actually blessed the murder of "subversives" as a necessity for preserving "Christian civilization." Belatedly, in 1995, senior Catholic bishops expressed remorse for not having done "more" to expose and stop this barbarity, when in fact they had done *nothing* to intervene and instead had actively sided with the military. How remarkable were Chile and Argentina in their respective responses to a fascist military government!

One night we managed to meet with a woman whose husband was "disappeared" and had been killed two years earlier. She in turn had been arrested, solely because her husband had been arrested. Her guard fell in love with her and brought her things to read. On her release he proposed to her, almost as if he had no sense of the torture that tiny cell had caused her. As a potter, she made a clay mobile of the things she most cherished while confined: sun, fish, a bell, birds, and a toilet. This she presented to June, a fellow potter, possibly because we would tell her story and end the damnable silence.

AUBURN THEOLOGICAL SEMINARY

Robert (Bob) Wood Lynn of the Union Theological Seminary faculty was overseeing the operation of a small continuing education and research center in the Union buildings, Auburn Theological Seminary, and took me on half-time. The other half was assumed by Hartford Seminary, which had closed shop as a degree-granting institution and was engaged in a project to improve church ministry. As Auburn grew under the inspired presidency of Barbara Wheeler, I was taken on full-time. Auburn gave me the freedom to innovate and independence from institutional responsibility. Thus began my new career as a roving leader of continuing education events.

Soon, June and I began to do workshops together, using not only clay and pastels, mime and role playing, but also her own unique blend of meditation and movement. Now I was doing what I wanted from the time of my experience in Oregon: to lead people in an encounter with Scripture that can be transformative. God, I felt, had been providentially at work in my being refused tenure at Union.

REFLECTION ON THE POWERS
from June 18, 1981

I am simply eager to get on with *The Powers'* books, yet I am afraid of failure too. I am afraid of not being able to pull it off as a total integrated work of art and thought. That is, of course, possible. But it is also the Devil undermining all chance of it happening as well. I want to learn again how to participate in that beauty, not to be separate, to commune again with angels. I experience God now as warmth, pleasure, growth, risk, thrust, ground, river, fullness, and wholeness.

DISCOVERING THE UNIVERSAL UNCONSCIOUS

One afternoon at the Guild for Psychological Studies, we all entered the pool as to a holy place. The leaders put on Jean Sibelius's *The Oceanides* and we were to move to the music with our eyes closed. At first I was inhibited, for my lifelong fear was of awkwardly falling down. But when I did, the water caught me. Suddenly I found myself cavorting around the pool, unafraid of falling. I was ecstatic. When the music stopped, and we opened our eyes, we dragged ourselves onto the pool side, amazed at what had happened. I realized that this composer had written music that had perfectly corresponded to my inner state. The composer and I were one. Here was a man on a different continent, in a different time, who described exactly the music of my soul. For years I had held at bay the universality of the unconscious. Here was living proof of its existence. And with it, I was able to take another step to letting go of my fear of falling, my fear of failure, and yet another step to becoming human.

I first attempted meditation as a sophomore in high school. I persevered, but I had to admit that little was happening. Meditation was the biggest waste of time I had ever known. That state of things continued right up to the present, but I had an experience that confirmed the value of meditation, if only I could get the hang of it.

Decades later, an ad crossed my desk announcing Buddhist retreats offered nearby. I seized upon the opportunity and went for a monthlong retreat. It was excruciating. We alternated forty-five-minute sessions seated and then the same amount of time walking, from 5:30 a.m. to 9:30 p.m., stopping only for meals and for my restless legs all night. Yet the harder I tried to clear the garbage out of my mind, the more fruitless the attempt became. Here was the chance of a lifetime to "clean house," and all I could produce was trivia.

By the end of the retreat, I felt utterly humiliated at my inability to jettison the junk that I had been passing off as "thought." Anything would be better than this. I knew in my deepest self that this was probably the last chance I would ever have to silence the mindless chatter that was choking my brain waves. So I signed on for a seven-day retreat a few weeks later.

More than once I asked myself if I was crazy. But I began to have moments of clarity. Then, on the sixth day, everything stopped—all the chatter, noise, striving, self-consciousness was gone. In its place was an exquisite peace. The racket was replaced by silence. This state of mind lasted for two and a half hours. Then, gradually, it subsided. Was this the state of satori? Does it matter? This was a gift from Buddhism to me, a Christian, and I was immensely grateful.

This retreat was held in what used to be a Roman Catholic monastery. The meditation took place in a large room, which one entered by means of an anteroom. In that anteroom there were still two stained-glass windows from its former Christian days: one of Jesus at the Last Supper, and the other one of Jesus in Gethsemane. Suddenly I realized I was lonely. Jesus was my buddy. No matter how wonderful the experience of satori was for me, it had to be correlated with Jesus. Not because Jesus was the best, but because he was simply *my* best. Could it be that Jesus was reminding me of the search for the Human Being inside me?

So I would go to the stained-glass windows and say, to the one, "Hi, Jesus," and to the other, "Hi, Jesus"—and then practice Buddhist meditation.

Mysticism has often been misunderstood as the attempt to escape this simple, phenomenal world to a more pure existence in heaven beyond. That is not mysticism, but Gnosticism. Biblical mysticism is the attempt to exit "this world," to an alternative reality that pervades the old order. Its goal is to jettison the mind-set that says "greed is good," "selfishness is normal," and "killing is necessary." Mysticism in biblical terms is not escapism, as so many have caricaturized it, but a fight for ethics and social change.

When we turn to the New Testament, we find that the phrase used in Ezekiel's vision, "the son of man," is also used there. What we seem to have is a mythic figure without a myth. It was the seminal contribution of Elizabeth Boyden Howes, following the lead of her mentor, Carl Jung, to recognize that "the son of the man" was not a title, or a nickname, or a circumlocution, or a myth, but an archetypal image. As an archetypal image, it functions as a symbol of wholeness, less august and almighty than the Messiah or Christ, more mundane and daily than the heroes of myth, more a catalytic agent of transformation in the service of the Self than a symbol of the Self as such.

Howes revealed to me the potential, theologically, of "the son of the man" in Ezekiel and the Gospels. Her seminal insights and her questioning method of exegesis are continued by the Guild for Psychological Studies.

It is impossible in the limits of this book to provide the exegetical grounding that alone would make that hypothesis persuasive. Briefly, I regard the so-called earthly "son of the man" sayings as, on the whole, reliable, though that has to be settled case by case. But it seems altogether implausible that a church that already was regarding Jesus as ascended to the right hand of the Power of God would then create sayings and stories that emphasize Jesus's lowliness. Likewise, while no extant prediction of the passion may be preserved verbatim, I do believe that Jesus said something like "the son of the man must suffer many things and be rejected."

One editorial statement by Matthew gives us rare insight into what at least one evangelist thought about "son of the man." In the story of the Healing of the Paralytic (Matt. 9:2–8), Jesus has just said that "the son of the man has authority on earth to forgive sins" (Matt. 9:6). In reporting the acclamation of the crowd, Matthew makes this astonishing statement: "and they glorified God, who had given such authority to"—and here we would expect Matthew of all people to finish the clause with "Christ" or at least "Jesus." Instead, he has "human beings" (Matt. 9:8). (The Hebrew equivalent would be *benei adam*.) The Human Being is not then restricted to Jesus, but includes his disciples and, indeed, anyone who is in relationship with the process of becoming whole. So also, in the plucking of grain on the Sabbath (Mark 2:23–28), it is not Jesus but the disciples who take upon themselves the right to decide when the Sabbath is being broken: "Then he said to them, 'The Sabbath was made for humankind, and not humankind for the Sabbath; so the son of the human being is lord even of the Sabbath'" (Mark 2:27–28).

Such sovereign freedom, placed in the hands of the underclasses, inevitably strikes terror in the hearts of those entrusted with the tranquility of society. The dramatic location of the initiation of the death plot against Jesus in Mark 3:6, only a few verses after the story of the plucking of the grain (Mark 2:23–28), may or may not be chronologically exact, but it is logically appropriate. It was not simply the religious and political authorities who trembled at the human cost of such freedom, however. The early church also blanched at so much moral discretion being placed at the disposal of common people. Hence Matthew and Luke omit Mark 2:27 ("the Sabbath was made for humankind . . ."). But verse 27 is the original connection to verses 23 and 24, since it alone responds to the initial controversy. By deleting that verse, Matthew and Luke have converted the saying into its opposite: the assertion that Jesus alone as "the son of man" is lord of the Sabbath. Once "the son of the man" had been flattened into a mere equivalent of Son of God and Christ/Messiah, no other reading seemed possible. Whereas special need had originally justified the breach or suspension of the law, now one's relationship with a special person does so—a person endowed with a transcendent authority shared by no one else.

God transcendent is God immanent in the human being. Jesus does not contemplate a God outside the universe intervening to heal the paralytic, but as a power which can be evoked in the sick person himself: "*Your* faith has made you whole" (Mark 10:52; and frequently). If through Jesus they had been put in touch with the human being within them, no wonder they had such collective self-confidence and indomitable courage. These lowly disciples of Jesus are authorized with a power that equals or exceeds that of the priesthood. And this power is not derivative. It is not conferred by heredity or ordination. It is directly from God. It is not even mediated by Jesus, though it is clearly evoked by him. "But so that you may know that *the son of the man* has authority on earth to forgive sins"—he said to the paralytic—"I say to you, stand up, take your mat and go to your home" (Mark 2:10–11).

To exercise the authority to forgive sins is to assume the power that one already has, but of which one is unaware. People are not just unaware, but deprived, systematically stripped of their own power by the power needs of those religious authorities who hold a monopoly on the dispensation of God's grace. To claim the power to forgive sins is thus not only to restore the lost humanity of others, but to recover lost aspects of one's own humanity as well.[*]

But when all authority is vested only in Jesus, what becomes of the sovereign freedom that Jesus evoked in his disciples? What becomes of deciding for ourselves what is right (Luke 12:57)? It is indeed awesome how Christology has been used to avoid Jesus's clear intent. So the astonishing freedom of the human being was sabotaged in the interests of institutional harmony and rule by law.

* For more detailed exegesis, see Walter Wink, *The Human Being: Jesus and the Enigma of the Son of the Man* (Minneapolis, MN: Fortress Press, 2001).

In Brazil, the military government gave up power but remained in the wings, ready to step in if they saw their interests threatened. Unlike other military governments that were summarily removed, as in Argentina, the Brazilian military slowly permitted a relaxation that resulted in the establishment of democracy after ten years. During that time, though, the slums in São Paulo and Rio de Janeiro were beyond imagination. Add to that the widespread murder of kids by the police as a crime-control strategy, and you have a recipe for disaster. Inflation merely made things worse.

In what has to be one of the most audacious nonviolent resistance moves ever made against a military dictatorship, a Presbyterian minister, Jaime Wright, with the complete support of São Paulo's cardinal, Paulo Evaristo Arns, managed the secret photocopying of the military's entire archive, documenting every detail of torture and every disappearance. In anticipation of democracy in 1979, the military proposed a blanket amnesty that would cover both those accused of political crimes and state security agents who were involved in human rights violations. Victims who had already served time and had been routinely tortured were to be lumped on a par with torturers and killers who had paid nothing for their crimes. This "clean start" would have meant, in reality, burying the past under a coat of sludge. But Rev. Wright's brother had "disappeared," and Rev. Wright was not about to accept silence.

That 1979 amnesty law, however, provided lawyers access to the archives, though only on a piecemeal basis, as they prepared amnesty petitions on behalf of their clients. Lawyers were allowed to take out individual files for a maximum of twenty-four hours. Wright and his lawyer colleagues hatched a plan to secretly copy these records. Cardinal Arns made it his personal concern, and offered to assume responsibility if anything went wrong. Philip Potter, the general secretary of the World Council of Churches, pledged clandestine financial support (which eventually reached $350,000).

Twelve lawyers began systematically checking out files from the archive on what they hoped would seem to be a random basis. Wright and his coconspirators leased three photocopying machines and employed staff to operate them for ten hours a day, seven days a week. This went on, undetected, for three years, when suddenly Wright realized that they had copied *the entire archive*—over a million pages! The secret was so complete that most of the people who had worked on the project didn't even know that they had been engaged in it, even when they later read the final report.

The copied files were regularly transferred from Brasília to São Paulo, where they were microfilmed. A courier was kept busy spiriting the microfilms out of the country, several dozen at a time, five hundred in all, as insurance in case the operation was discovered. Repeatedly, at the merest hint that their secrecy had been breached, the entire operation would be transferred to another hideout provided in some obscure church building by Cardinal Arns. Meanwhile, the million photocopied pages were being boiled down to a seven-thousand-page report, which was then further condensed to a summary digest that was secretly printed. Then one day in the summer of 1985, the digest suddenly appeared on bookstands all over the nation under the title *Brasil: Nunca Mais* (*Brazil: Never Again, Torture in Brazil* [Austin: University of Texas Press, 1998]). It created a sensation.

The military still possessed total veto power, even as it was handing over control to civilians. In 1980, they canceled elections, and as late as April 1984, the Army suddenly took over the streets of Brasília in a show of force. The military wanted everyone to know that there could be no nullification of the blanket amnesty and no prosecution of human rights violators. So Brazilians had to be content with the full disclosure of truth that *Brasil: Nunca Mais* provided.

Normally, truth commissions do not have access to the dictatorship's records and must take the testimony of hundreds of people. Making that testimony public runs the risk of falsely accusing persons who then have no recourse to a trial to clear their names. The brilliance of the Brazilian exposure was that no one was incriminated by the testimony of victims, but rather by the factual reports of the military's own recorders. In Brazil, not only was prosecution of torturers impossible, but the new civil government itself never endorsed the *Brasil: Nunca Mais* report. But knowing the truth was, in itself, a kind of victory over the powers of repression. And for many people, knowing the truth is itself liberating.

The G8 is a self-appointed rich countries' club made up of the wealthiest nations of the world who have been authorized by no one but themselves. Demonstrations at various economic summits, such as the G8, were getting more and more violent. The G8 meeting in Genoa, Italy, in 2001 had led to the loss of a life and over one hundred people injured during massive rioting. Things looked worse in 2004 for the upcoming summit in Brunswick, Georgia, the poorest zip code in America.

Well before the event, the media advised motorists that roadblocks and security checkpoints on bridges and highways would cause major traffic delays, and suggested that local residents plan to take their vacations during the week of the G8 Summit to avoid the inconvenience. Those who planned to stay in town were advised to remain indoors— for their own safety. In response to the possibility of an al Qaeda attack, every public school and college in coastal Georgia was ordered closed "for security purposes." All postal delivery was canceled. Should churches desire to organize events during the G8 Summit, they were asked to hold prayer vigils for the G8 leaders. Virtually every conference venue and lodging was either placed off-limits "for security reasons" or booked by the federal government to house the twenty thousand CIA, FBI, Homeland Security, Secret Service, Army National Guard, or state and local police. This made it virtually impossible to secure a venue. Not until five days before the counterconference did the governor of Georgia finally cave in and give access to Coastal Georgia Community College.

Since the government had bought up every room for miles around, we had to sleep in a motel under reconstruction, without hall lights. The law enforcement officers conspicuously patrolled communities all along the coast from Savannah to the Florida border. Some of the vehicles driving by the church had machine guns mounted on them, which the gunners sometimes trained on the demonstrators. There was talk of nineteen flatbed trucks loaded with missiles traveling down I-95.

The police periodically strutted their stuff on the streets—driving in long motorcades for no apparent reason, lights flashing, sometimes followed by vans of heavily equipped troops. Helicopters and fighter jets conspicuously patrolled the sky. Newscasts were spiced with stories about the arrival of two thousand body bags and reserved refrigeration capacity to hold them when necessary. In the days leading up to the G8 Summit, broadcasters alluded to martial law and the possibility of a curfew.

In the face of this federal onslaught, many had qualms about attending. We had expected five thousand people, as at previous sessions; instead, there were, at most, a few hundred.

Despite all these attempts at intimidation, I was able to deliver the plenary address and lead the workshop, both on nonviolence, to a receptive audience. The ridiculous lengths to which the authorities went in order to prevent the violence experienced in Genoa, and elsewhere, was tolerated by the public because people felt threatened. But it was a fear manufactured by the authorities. The great demonstrations in Washington, New York, and elsewhere, in fact, all over the world, have been largely nonviolent. The fact that "The Other Economic Summit" (as our protest was named) chose a nonviolent path indicated that we had learned our lesson, and that nonviolence would be our mode of operation from here on. It is urgent that we teach nonviolence as a "third way" that can ultimately spread peace in the world.

SOUTH AFRICA

Witnessing the effectiveness of nonviolence in the Americas—from Selma to São Paulo—and observing it in Jesus's own teachings, I became increasingly convinced that nonviolence was the only way to overcome the domination of the Powers without creating new forms of domination. I had seen how asserting our autonomy over the Powers can bring us closer to God without, in turn, trying to subjugate the oppressors and declare revenge. I decided to test this hunch in South Africa.

One encounter became emblematic to me of the inhumanity of apartheid. I recall a scene at the Crossroads squatters' camp in which a teenage girl vomited a foot-long worm. What a metaphor for a society on the brink of violent revolution! But violence wouldn't work, that much was clear to me. I knew there was another way, if only the leadership of the land could embrace it. Given the nature of apartheid, the only thing that I could do to help was to write. When I returned from South Africa, the book almost wrote itself. It wound up being *Jesus' Third Way* (Philadelphia: New Society Publishers, 1987), later titled *Violence and Nonviolence in South Africa*. In it, I urged the churches of South Africa to become more involved in nonviolent direct action against the apartheid regime. With the financial help of the Fellowship of Reconciliation (FOR), our little Monterey UCC church in the Berkshires of Massachusetts individually addressed three thousand one hundred copies to the black and white English-speaking clergy of South Africa. Later, the South African Roman Catholic church sent out another eight hundred copies to its clergy.

The book infuriated some; how dare a white American male tell those who are already suffering to suffer more, voluntarily and deliberately. Even more anger came from those committed to a violent solution. But it had its intended effect. Someone from the outside had to say what few within could say, without losing credibility. The book redefined nonviolence. What was previously understood as nonresistance and passivity, unfortunately thanks to the white missionaries, turned into militant action, and did so by appeal to Jesus's own teaching. Within a year, the debate had completely reversed itself (my book was only one of a number of factors) and the head of the South African Council of Churches, Frank Chikane, was calling on the churches to engage in active nonviolence.

In 1988, Richard Deats of the Fellowship of Reconciliation and I were invited to do workshops on nonviolence in South Africa. When the government refused to issue me a visa, the person who had invited me, Rob Robertson, suggested that I try to enter illegally. First, Richard Deats (who could get a visa, not having been to South Africa before) and I led a workshop on nonviolence in Lesotho (which we could enter without a visa). At worship each morning, we sang:

Thine be the glory,
Risen, conquering Son!
Endless is the victory
Thou o'er death hast won.

Someone had made a large wooden cross from a couple of planks about eight feet high and four feet wide, and during the service participants were asked to affix their names to it. The name-bearing cross would have provided the police with a ready-made roster of those apprehended in a raid. Hence the act of placing one's name upon a cross during a service of worship signified: "I am a person who is willing to suffer in the struggle against apartheid."

The act further signified: "Not only am I willing in principle to suffer and risk for the sake of opposing apartheid, but I do put myself at risk here and now, by giving up the possibility of remaining anonymous on this occasion."

It struck me how powerfully Paul's words spoke to the occasion:

> For we are not contending against flesh and blood, but against the principalities, against the powers, against the world rulers of this present darkness, against the spiritual hosts of wickedness in the heavenly places (RSV Eph. 6:12).
>
> ... That through the church the manifold wisdom of God might now be made known to the principalities and powers in the heavenly places (RSV Eph. 3:9–10).

> He disarmed the principalities and powers
> and made a public example of them (RSV Col.
> 2:15).

The workshop ended with a final service of worship. We asked each participant to write down on a piece of construction paper the name of the particular power that had him or her most in its thrall. Our aim was to provide an occasion for persons to become conscious of the Powers that prevent, or try to prevent, their being faithful to the Kingdom of God in their own South African context. People wrote phrases like "Fear of Death," "Fear of Torture," "Separation from Family," and "Fear of Detention." Holding these insignia aloft, the people now formed a procession, at the head of which was the great cross with their names attached. The procession circled the room and sang:

> *Thine be the glory,*
> *Risen, conquering Son!*
> *Endless is the victory*
> *Thou o'er death hast won.*

The tune was from Handel's *Judas Maccabeus*. When the procession and the hymn ended, the cross with its names attached was placed against a wall. Participants carried the sign bearing the names of the Powers they feared to the coal stove and burned them. Someone said a prayer, and the event was over.

Buoyed by the prayers of many people, Rob and I drove

to the border crossing that Rob thought would give us the best chance of entering South Africa. Suddenly the sky turned black. As we came in sight of the border we stopped and prayed that, as God had opened the prison doors and let Peter and Paul and Silas out, God would let us in! Then in the pouring rain, we drove up to the border post, jumped out, and ran under the shelter of the porch, where the senior soldier in charge was whistling, "Thine is the glory, risen, conquering Son. . . ." Instantly I knew we were in. The rain-darkened room was so dim that I literally had to read our passports to the other soldier; he never even looked for a visa. We drove to Johannesburg and did nonviolence workshops for a week, and then we went to Pretoria and turned me in.

Without an appointment, we entered the appropriate building, rode the elevator, sailed by the secretaries, and walked unannounced into the offices of the Ministry of Home Affairs—which handles visas! I introduced myself.

"Hi, I'm Professor Walter Wink."

"You can't be!" he thundered. "I have your file right here on my desk." (Sure enough, there it was, all alone on his desk, two inches thick.)

"How did you get here?"

He was so upset that he forgot to press his question. And then, in one of those reversals frequent in bureaucrats the world over, he remembered that he was in charge of people entering the country, but if we were already there, we were no longer under his jurisdiction. So he relaxed, even sharing jokes with us. I asked if I could stay until my flight was scheduled. He agreed, but checked it with his superior, who was furious and ordered me out of the country immediately. When we got to the airport, we were greeted most cordially by a Mr. Gideon, who wanted to give me the redcarpet treatment by bumping me to the head of the line, but I wanted to savor every last minute with my friends. The authorities must have been so embarrassed that I had gotten in that they passed me off as a business tycoon or something.

Later, the cabinet minister of Home Affairs wrote Rob:

> The way Prof. Wink entered South Africa is not acceptable and is considered in a serious light. In this connection your attention is also invited to the provisions of section 51 of the abovementioned Act in terms of which it is an offence to aid or abet any person in entering or remaining in the Republic in contravention of the Act. Such person is liable on conviction to a fine not exceeding R10,000 or to imprisonment for a period not exceeding five years or both that fine and that imprisonment.
>
> In future, when planning to visit the RSA, Prof Wink must apply in the prescribed way for a visa and await the outcome before proceeding to South Africa.

Catch-22: It was their refusal of a visa that led to my illegal entry!

LETTER FROM SOUTH AFRICA

One of the most courageous opponents of apartheid, Methodist Bishop of South Africa Peter Storey, later wrote this about my book, *Jesus' Third Way,* and it remains one of the most flattering and meaningful responses to my work:

> It is a great joy to recall what [the book] meant to us in South Africa. It came in a plain brown wrapper, and its cover bore no publisher's mark or illustration—simply the title, *Jesus' Third Way.* This particular edition had been prepared for those of us struggling to witness God's justice in apartheid South Africa, especially those trapped between rejecting the brutality of violence and the guilt of doing nothing. The book's plain exterior was designed to raise the least possible suspicious interest on the part of our Security Police, but inside the covers were one hundred pages of carefully thought-through revolution. Walter Wink's analysis of the prospects of violence and nonviolence in the anti-apartheid struggle were uncompromising; they let none of us off—proponents of violence and nonviolence alike. He chided us gently for our hypocrisy and

146

impotence and showed us that the true realism lay, as we should have known, not with "fight" or "flight," but with Jesus and his "Third Way" of nonviolent direct action. Informed by the Gospels as well as by the hard math of the struggle, Walter invited us to follow the tough advice and the example of Jesus in confronting the powers with a different kind of power. He reminded us of other struggles where the odds were stacked just as heavily against freedom, but where people trained in the Third Way of Jesus had overcome.

The logic of Wink's Bible studies was devastating: Far from counseling passivity, Jesus in the Sermon on the Mount was inviting us to a loving, determined subversion of our enemies. Provided we were willing to bring to our struggle an even greater courage than that expected of people of force, in the Gospels we had in our hands something much more potent than any weapons of insurrection. *Jesus' Third Way* grew out of Walter Wink's own confrontation with South Africa's powers in 1986 and both that visit and his publication in 1987 came at a crucial time for us. A weary church, stung by the Kairos Document, was turning to half-hearted endorsements of an "armed struggle" that it never really believed in and which had not the slightest hope of prevailing over apartheid's armies. We needed to rediscover our unique role—to be nerved to be church again.

South Africa is free now, liberated not by armed battalions but by millions of ordinary people refusing to collaborate any longer in their own oppression, and doing so largely non-violently. The book in the plain brown wrapper helped us believe that this could happen and showed us where to look to see it happening already, inviting us to join what God was doing.

ON DYING

from January 4, 2011

From June: Walter had a deep sense of urgency about this book. He knew his disease was degenerative and that time was short. In the afternoon, after a nap, Walter came out of his room confused. He went to shave but instead picked up a book.

I said to him, "You are sad. What are you feeling?"

"I am going to miss you so much," he answered. We talked about death and dying, and who is left.

I said, "I may be the one who dies first."

"Chances are 100 to 1 that won't happen," he said.

"I will be the lonesome one. You will be fine," I assured him. Walter broke down and cried and cried.

I said, "Do you feel better?"

He nodded his head yes. Of course, we hugged tightly, as we always did.

PAUL COMES OUT

One night June and I were awakened by the tear-racked voice of June's cousin Paul, calling from Maine. We could tell by the sound of his voice that he was in desperate need. It didn't take long for him to quickly and directly utter, "June, I need to talk to you. May I come see you?"

Upon Paul's arrival, he and June immediately went walking. For a time Paul couldn't speak. June, sensing the turmoil Paul was experiencing, stopped and turned to him and simply said, "Paul, you're gay!" Now the tears were torrential. He had had fifty-four years of dissembling: dating women to give the impression of heterosexuality, then when they began to get serious, breaking off the relationship for no apparent reason. And then there was the danger of blowing his cover at work. Paul had been a close part of our family for years, and although it was apparent to all of us what his sexual orientation was, the subject was never broached. He had never had a sexual relationship. What was amazing here is that Paul never had a clue that anyone thought of him in any other way but heterosexual. We loved Paul, and we felt honored to help him come out.

Once back in Maine, one of the first things he did was

to attend his community church. Being eager to announce to the world his new freedom to be himself, he turned to the man sitting beside him in the pew and blurted out, "I'm gay." The man paused and with a sense of trust replied, "You know, my son is gay also. Thank you for sharing."

When I was in junior high I was "adopted" by a seminary student who was going blind. He must have been in his late twenties. We were close to inseparable. Other people snickered behind our backs, but our relationship was so—pure—that people just dropped it. At some level I knew he was gay, though I blocked any expression of it.

Later, when the issue of gay rights heated up, I made no connection between my earlier relationship with Jay and the furor over gay rights. In several cases, I made comments that were downright derogatory toward gays. My Union Seminary students straightened me out on that. Union was a hotbed of courageous women and men willing to step out of their closets and declare to the community and the world that they were lesbians and gays and not ashamed of it. This awareness was not only an education we all needed but a genuine bonding of the community for professors and students alike.

In 1979, I was asked by the New York Conference of the United Methodist Church to do a biblical analysis of the whole issue of homosexuality. I think it was one of the most objective pieces I have ever written. When I tried in vain to get my essay published, June and I published it out of our own pockets, and the Fellowship of Reconciliation agreed to distribute it.

The gist of my essay is this: The Bible has no sexual ethic. Instead, it exhibits a variety of sexual mores, some of which changed over the thousand-year span of biblical history. Mores are unreflective customs accepted by a given community. Many of the practices that the Bible prohibits, we allow, and many that it allows, we prohibit. The Bible knows only a love ethic, which is constantly being brought to bear on whatever sexual mores are dominant in any given country, or culture, or period.

For instance, virtually all modern readers would agree with the Bible in rejecting:

> Incest
> Rape
> Adultery
> Intercourse with animals

But we disagree with the Bible on most other sexual mores. The Bible condemned the following behaviors, which we generally allow:

> Intercourse during menstruation
> Celibacy (some texts)
> Exogamy (marriage with non-Israelites)
> Naming sexual organs
> Nudity (under certain conditions)
> Masturbation (some Christians still condemn this)
> Birth control (some Christians still forbid this)

And the Bible regarded semen and menstrual blood as unclean, which most of us do not. Likewise, the Bible permitted behaviors that we today condemn:

> Prostitution
> Polygamy
> Levirate marriage
> Sex with slaves
> Concubinage (cohabiting without marriage)
> Treatment of women as property
> Very early marriage (for the girl, age 11–13)

And while the Old Testament accepted divorce, Jesus forbade it. In short, of the sexual mores mentioned here, we only agree with the Bible on four of them, and disagree with it on sixteen!

So we must critique the sexual mores of any given time by the love ethic exemplified by Jesus. Augustine already dealt with this in his inspired phrase, "Love God, and do as you please." This doesn't mean everything goes. It means that everything is to be critiqued by Jesus's love commandment.

Where the Bible mentions homosexual behavior at all, it clearly condemns it. I freely grant that. The issue is precisely whether the biblical judgment is correct. The Bible sanctioned slavery as well, and nowhere attacked it as unjust. Yet today, if you were to ask Christians in the South whether the Bible sanctions slavery, virtually everyone would agree that it does not. How do we account for such a monumental shift? The same goes for the changing role of women in churches. The way out, however, is not to deny the presence of the sexism in Scripture, but to develop an interpretive theory that judges even Scripture in the light of the revelation of Jesus. What Jesus gives us is a critique of domination in all its forms, a critique that can be turned on the Bible itself. The Bible thus contains the principles of its own correction. We are freed from bibliolatry, the worship of the Bible. It is restored to its proper place as witness to the Word of God. And that word is a Person, not a book. The issue is not moral but "hermeneutical," that is, a matter of how we interpret Scripture. Our cowardice in facing that fact is at the heart of the conflict.

With the interpretive grid provided by a critique of domination, we are able to filter out the sexism, patriarchalism, violence, and homophobia that are very much a part of the Bible, thus liberating it to reveal to us in fresh ways the inbreaking, in our time, of God's domination-free order.

Now, as to gay marriage, in 1 Corinthians 7:7 Paul describes marriage as a "charisma" ("gift," tantamount to "vocation"), and urges his correspondents to stay single, as he is. Don't marry unless you have a vocation for it, he says, or because you are "burning" with sexual energy that you aren't sure you can contain. In 1 Corinthians 7:36–38 Paul admits that this is just his opinion or advice. With a 50 percent rate of heterosexual divorce in the United States today, it would appear that a great many people don't have the "gift" of marriage. In any case, gays and lesbians certainly ought to have the same opportunity to fail or succeed at marriage!

This raises a question of hypocrisy, evasion, and moral cowardice. Hypocrisy, because the churches are willing to let the states provide the legal rights and privileges for which their own lesbian and gay members yearn, and are denied in their churches. Evasion, because the churches have condemned gays and lesbians for having a promiscuous lifestyle, while denying them access to the one institution in society that fosters marital fidelity. And moral cowardice, because the churches are willing to sacrifice members of their own flocks in order to avoid controversy, conflict, and possible schism.

RETIREMENT

I have often wondered if there would be any outcome to my ministry. Of course, I knew that some people were helped, even transformed, by the Spirit, because they wrote or called to say so. But the outpouring of love at my retirement was beyond any of my expectations. All of us should have such an event before, rather than after, our deaths.

Between all of my travels, Auburn Theological Seminary was like an oasis, where I was a camel in the desert. On the road, I lacked the stimulation that only one's colleagues can provide. Auburn was like a theological think tank. How many people are fortunate enough to have the rich experience of such interesting and brilliant colleagues?

It doesn't seem possible that thirty-five years have passed. Time snuck up on me and all of the sudden, here I am, retired. I have tried to make something productive of my time. I have tried to write, to enrich theological education.

KIRKBRIDGE

April 6, 1994

I sit—wine-warmed—
my mind all a-drizzle, as the fog
like a tea cozy covers
the earth. The evening
plants its wet kiss
on the tree and road. And my soul,
dripping with mist,
climbs into God's lap, curling into a ball,
dreams of becoming.

ASCENSION

Jesus is depicted as having ascended to the right hand of the Power of God. If we read this literally, as if Jesus rode a sunbeam back to God's throne room in the sky, it is virtually unintelligible. If, however, we take it as the accurate report of an archetypal mutation, it makes perfect sense. Something new had come to birth in the collective and personal psyches of the disciples. The human being whose divine power and authority they had seen incarnate in Jesus, and occasionally in themselves, had now entered the heart of reality as a catalyst in the process of human transformation. The ascension is not grist for the discussion of miracles, because it was not a miracle. It marks an actual change in some people's perception of the divine. To see the human being ascended is thus to set our sights on what it means to become a human being. The human being "at the right hand of Power" is the future of the species. "Seeing" this is to recognize that the human being as lived out by Jesus has entered the collective consciousness of humanity. Now it has become an archetypal image, capable of galvanizing unlived life and mobilizing untapped resistance to the institutions and structures that squeeze life out of people. Picturing heaven as "up" is, of course, merely a convention of thought. But it well captures the sense that this figure, exalted from ignominious execution, shame, and abandonment, has become the "highest" value in the universe, the criterion of value itself, and the revelation of humanity's evolutionary goal, as Teilhard de Chardin saw so clairvoyantly. The slogan for this hope is that stunning passage in 1 John 3:2—"Beloved, we are God's children now; what we will be has not yet been revealed. What we do know is this: when human being is revealed, we will be like him, for we will see him as he is."

For his disciples, Jesus's death and ascension were like a black hole in space that sucked into its collapsing vortex the very meaning of the universe, until in the intensity of its compaction there was an explosive reversal, and the stuff of which galaxies are made was blown out into the universe. So Jesus's ascension to the right hand of the Power of God was a supernova in the archetypal sky. As the image of the truly Human One, Jesus became an exemplar of our own utmost possibilities for living.

The image of God, and other related images, thus underwent fundamental mutation. Jesus, as it were, infiltrated the Godhead. The very image of God was altered by the sheer force of Jesus's being. God was, in Jesus, taking on a human face. God would never be the same. Jesus indelibly imprinted the divine; God everlastingly entered the human. Following Jung, we might say that in Jesus, God took on humanity, furthering the evolution revealed in Ezekiel's vision of Yahweh on the throne in "the likeness, as it were, of human form" (Ezek. 1:26). From now on, Jesus's followers would experience God through the filter of Jesus. Jesus, people realized during his lifetime, is like God. God, they realized after his death, is now like Jesus. It is merely a prejudice of modern thought that events happen only in the outer world. What Christians regard as the most significant event in human history happened, according to the Gospels, in the psychic realm—and it altered our history irrevocably.

I have had a wonderful life. I have been paid to do what I most like to do: interpreting Scripture, which I have been doing at a furious pace, leading workshops on the Bible with June hither and yon, our suitcases always at the ready. Interpreting Scriptures is what I do best, and most. I am never so happy as I am when I rise to Scripture's challenge. As I once commented, it has been the most fruitful and exciting journey of my life. Now comes the test I initially set before us: Does knowing something of a person's life story make possible a deeper understanding of the biblical text and of its interpreters? Does an "autobiography of my interest in Jesus" yield insights that would otherwise remain unavailable? The answer may appear self-evident, but it is not. Scholars and preachers alike ignore the insights that come from opening our souls to the Human Being. The vast majority of biblical scholars still work from an objectivist stance. But there has nevertheless been a considerable shift.

APOCALYPTIC

On the other hand, the human being in the formalized sense was literalized into the apocalyptic notion of the second coming of the "son of the man." The human being is no longer seen as present and future. Rather, the human being is drenched with the symbolism of a longed-for wholeness in an indefinite future. The human being has become numinous, coming like a flash of lightning that illumines the sky from one end of heaven to the other (Matt. 24:27; Luke 17:24). The power and glory of the human being are fearsome, and the judgments of the human being are categorical. All these "son of the man" aspects, says Jung, are mythic, collective, unconscious, and, as such, unrelated to individual consciousness. Forgiveness will not be a part of this final, future judgment. There will be no loving enemies. The "son of the man" has lost all contact with the earth. Everything now takes place in the sky. The deep archetypal movement of images from the depth are pulled out and projected on a transcendent spiritual world, as if on a cosmic screen. The urgency of deciding for or against the new order of Jesus has not become a call for unlimited and unending watchfulness, ". . . for the son of the man is coming at an hour you do not expect" (Matt.

24:44; Luke 12:40). The "son of the man" is identified with the figure of the Judge of all the world, whose judgments separated sheep from goats, for an otherworldly heaven and hell (Matt. 25:31–46). On his return, Jesus would do all the things he resolutely refused to do the first time around. Jesus would come again as ruler, using all necessary force to coerce humanity into obedience to the divine purposes. It appears that God's immortal patience will have finally run out, and that all the weapons in the arsenal of righteousness will be used to devastating effect by the Supreme Commander of the heavenly hosts. This heavenly "son of the man" is a long, long way from the Galilean teacher who renounced violence in the name of a nonviolent God.

Thus depersonalized and deprived of real immediacy, the human being dropped from devotional life and from the life of the church generally. Reference to the "son of the man" disappeared from the church's creeds and liturgies like a stone in a lake.

It appears that the public was not ready for the human being that Jesus knew and called others to relate to. Soon after his death, these aspects fell again into the unconscious and were projected onto the divine Christ. But the apocalypticization of the gospel served an important purpose, nevertheless. It held the urgency of the human being's "coming," as it were, in suspension, preserving the potential of the human being for future generations. The apocalyptic gospel has permanently preserved the unconscious contents of the psyche in "constellated" form, ready at any time to erupt into consciousness. Consequently, all through the history of the church we see new outbreaks of creative energy and vision, as the virtual possibilities are made concrete and actual by fresh seers and prophets. But when archetypal contents are allowed to remain unconscious, violent explosions of murderous zeal follow: crusades, pogroms, inquisitions, holy wars, persecutions, and anti-Semitism. Such a time is upon us.

The human being wants to happen in and among us. The human being wants to be lived in our reality. There is something dynamic in that movement, but rather than see that dynamism within, the church placed it outside the self in an historical future. Thus the delay of the coming of "the son of the man," which after two thousand years can be considered not a delay but a failed and misplaced hope. The second coming is like a runner preserved in glass. The runner is running, but it is going nowhere.

I do not wish to leave the impression that the apocalyptic "son of the man" sayings are valueless. I believe that Jesus did look for the final triumph of God in history, he did await an actual realm of justice and peace, he felt the urgency of this new reality pressing into the world all the time, and he lived "as if" that new order was already beginning to dawn. And we can also see that the followers of Jesus were learning to incarnate the "possible human." Solidarity and even identity between Jesus and his disciples began during his ministry, as the hypothetical document "Q" saying suggests: "Whoever welcomes you welcomes me, and whoever welcomes me welcomes the one who sent me" (Matt. 10:40; parallel, Luke 10:16).

As T. W. Manson put it, the disciples can represent Jesus in the fullest sense because they, together with him, are a corpus, the son of the man, the embodiment of the remnant idea in Israel, the organ of God's redemptive purpose in the world. When the early church regarded the ascended human being as encompassing true humanness, which included Jesus and all others in whom the human being was alive, they were simply continuing on a new level the partnership they had as *shaliachim*, those sent out in the name of their master.

Thus, Jesus's followers did not just speak in the name of the human being, but as the human being. They could speak with the full authority of the human being because they were the human being speaking. They could heal and cast out demons, not because they had been authorized to do so by the human being, but because they were the human being healing and exorcising. They could declare sins forgiven without the necessity of sacrifice and temple, not because they had been commissioned to do so by the human being, but because they were the human being forgiving. Like Jesus, they too had no place to lay their heads; as such, they were living the unsettled life of the human being. Like Jesus, they had early on discovered their own sovereign freedom to decide what is right (Luke 12:57); as such, they were exercising the divine authority of the human being. Paul said as much when he spoke of the solidarity of redeemed humanity in Jesus as the Second Adam (Rom. 5:12–21).

A number of scholars argue that Jesus did not identify

with the coming "son of the man." For my part, I see the situation as a bit more complicated. Just as he did with the messianic hope, Jesus could neither identify himself without remainder with the "son of the man," nor deny that he was living out the "son of the man" in history. So at times, he could speak of the human being as indistinguishable from himself (Matt. 11:19; Luke 7:34), and at other times treat the human being as a corporate entity in which not only he but the disciples (Mark 2:23–28 parallels) and even outsiders could participate (Mark 9:38–41; Luke 9:49–50). The human being is more than simply Jesus; it represents the future of all humanity, indeed, the whole world, in the purposes of God (Rom. 8:18–25). Thus, during his active ministry on earth, Jesus could virtually identify with the human being (while including his disciples occasionally as well), because it was he who was incarnating it and constellating it as an image of transformation. Jesus became the Human Being without remainder, but the human being remained more than Jesus. Logically, A equals B, but B is more than A, with A being Jesus and B being the human being. After his death, resurrection, and ascension (and I regard the ascension as a psychic fact on the imaginal plane, not an historical event of the everyday world), the human being "seated at the right hand of the Power of God" became universal. As an archetypal image, as we noted earlier, the human being now mediates the possibility of becoming more fully human in the image and likeness of God, the Truly Human One. The human being is a catalytic agent for transformation, providing the form, lure, and hunger to become who we are truly meant to be or, more properly perhaps, to become who we truly are.

Why then did the expression "the son of the man" go so quickly into eclipse? We can now attempt an answer. The early church as reflected in the community that produced the hypothetical document "Q" saw its task as what Jesus taught about the human being. Thus they continued the ministry of Jesus, perpetuating in their own teaching, healing, and exorcism the same sovereign authority that Jesus had exercised and had extended to his disciples during his earthly ministry. Without ever completely abandoning that task, the church increasingly regarded Jesus's cross and resurrection as central. Now the focus was not on carrying forward Jesus's critique of domination, his healing and exorcism, and his liberative acts on behalf of those crushed by the Domination System. Rather, the focus became the worship of Jesus as sole divine bearer of salvation.

Some of us have become convinced that we not only do not need any longer to worship Jesus, but that we need to not worship him. As Revelations 22:9 laconically asserts, "Worship God." What we sense as the imperative of the gospel today is to continue Jesus's mission, to unmask the Domination System and to liberate those being crushed by it, to open people's lives to the living presence of God, and to foster the process of individuation as we seek to become the people we were meant to be. In that process, Jesus will continue to be the human representation of the human being, without being completely identified with it. The child of the Human One incarnated by Ezekiel, seen to be entering Godhead in Daniel 7:13, and lived into human flesh by Jesus, continues to beckon us in the form of the human Jesus, who had the courage to shoulder a unique revelation of the Mystery into concrete life. Just Jesus.

Just Jesus.

Just Jesus.

MY PSALM

Winds are blowing off the coast—
Chill winds, bracing to the soul.
A fine rain spines my face
Looking seaward toward the blast.

It is time. I hear the words
Like a harbor bell.
It is time to dare, to go beyond.

I have worked the field,
Plowed it up and down,
Planted, cultivated.
The harvest is coming in.

Now the sea calls.
The rocks along the shore
Rear against the crash.
Slithering rivulets of spent waves
Run to sea, calling.
Follow.

The Deep is in my nose.
Give me sea-legs and compass
To find my way Mariner.
I am aching for a cruise.

Acknowledgments

"In a sequel I will search for clues about how to become more human." This is the statement Walter wrote in the preface of his book titled *The Human Being*.

Many people along the way had asked him to do a shorter, simpler version of the *Human Being* book. But upon sitting down with an editor at Fortress Press to discuss this option, he was advised that it would be a difficult and a daunting task to condense the rich, detailed thesis of that book into a "digest" version without losing the depth. Walter accepted the recommendation and immediately set about writing his own personal stories as he scrutinized his own life experiences. Almost as if he were looking through a microscope, he began to observe clues that were the most powerful influences in his life.

Thus his book was conceived and brought to fruition through his last years.

Without the support of Steve Berry, this book would not have made it to press. There were endless hours and even days moving back and forth from Manchester, Vermont, to Sandisfield, Massachusetts, and from Sandisfield to Manchester, which provided the assurance Walter needed that his last book would be published. Steve and Carol Berry extended their home, their food, and their help in so many ways, creating a growing friendship of love and admiration. It is with genuine gratitude that I wish to thank Steve for the many hours of research, for his dedication, and for his patience. Steve explored many of the influential mentors who influenced Walter's academic journey. He was committed to focus on the task of finding out from various sources the fullness of Walter's life journey.

Often the three of us sat with Walter's journal in hand asking him if we might include this prayer or that reflection in his manuscript. He would shake his head in the affirmative. Other pieces were taken from workshops we led, where he participated in the related activities.

To all those who have read whole or even parts of Walter's stories, I would like to express gratitude just as Walter would be doing if it were possible for him to do so today. All were helpful in encouraging Walter to reflect on his own life stories. Gretchen Loral Startle devoted a long plane ride entirely to reading the beginning of the manuscript, reporting being sparked with excitement. Sheila and Dennis Linn were passionate that Walter gave from the depth of his soul. Thelma Jean Goodrich brought not only a psychological critique but also an objective compassion. In addition, Val Coleman, Mac Simms, and Owen deRis offered helpful comments.

Visitors came and went reading parts or the whole of the book. Many times we read Walter's stories out loud. Because they touched the hearers' own lives, they began to tell their own stories. Thank you, Michael and Lorri Harding, Tom Goodhue, Karen Pohlig, and Mel and Barbara Schlachter, to name a few. For those whose names I have mistakenly neglected to mention, please fill in your own name here. You were all a pillow of love.

To all the members of the South County Quaker Meeting in Great Barrington, Massachusetts, whose loving words and hands guided Walter, giving him encouragement throughout his diminishing abilities, I thank you from the bottom of my heart. Many close friends gave tremendous gifts of companionship, creating new stories beyond the closing of these written pages.

It was Barbara Morrison who stole Walter's devotion when she became his "buddy" day after day as caretaker. Rosanne Hoekstra brought smiles and laughter throughout her supporting role as helper. Special thanks to Courtney Bourns, whose deep friendship with Walter became even stronger during their regular "field trips" on the back roads of the beautiful Berkshires the last year of Walter's life.

A special thanks to Gareth Higgins, who opened the doors to the Crown Publishing Group through Trace Murphy, and eventually led to excellent editors.

In the end it was Dwayne Huebner, Tom Cole, and Wayne Rollins who were able to so correctly understand that Walter's own words were the sacred gems that reflected the essence of who he was; thus all stories and reflections are authentic as written by Walter. Only editorial corrections and fragments are additions.

I want to thank Bishop Peter Storey of South Africa for giving permission to use the letter he wrote to Walter concerning his book *Violence and Nonviolence in South Africa*.

Fortress Press has been magnanimous and generous in

allowing quotes from *The Human Being* to be freely used. I would like to personally pour my appreciation for the gracious manner in which Gary Jansen was open to talking to Walter when Walter just wanted to make sure his book was being remembered. I would also like to make a note of how available Gary was to me when I called him along the way for his guidance.

Amanda O'Connor, the editor I worked closely with, was extremely available to my fumbling ways of conveying what I would like to appear in the book. Her wisdom and expertise guided me through many queries. I am so grateful to Amanda for her openness, listening skills, and kind understanding of me as a novice.

I take full responsibility for the insistence that the stories be true to Walter's words only, knowing there were complete portions that for one reason or another did not make it into the book.

And, finally, the substance of our lives, our children: Steven Wink, Catherine Cook, Chris Wink, Jen Wink, Rebecca Wink, Tom Barnes, Kim Bergland, Tricia Bergland, Kurt Bergland, and Kathy White. And the joy of our lives, the grandchildren: Christian Bergland, Max Wink, Jack Wink, Carson Russo, Sona Wink, Lucy Barnes, Oliver Barnes, and Indy Wink.

To all I give thanks!

—*June Keener Wink*

About the Author

DR. WALTER WINK (1935–2012) was an influential American biblical scholar, theologian, and activist, and was an important figure in progressive Christianity. He was well known for his advocacy of, and work related to, nonviolent resistance. Wink earned his Ph.D. at the Union Theological Seminary, where he taught for nine years and in 2010 was honored with the Unitas Distinguished Alumni Award. He went on to spend much of his career teaching at Auburn Theological Seminary in New York City. Wink wrote more than sixteen books as well as hundreds of scholarly articles, and is recognized for coining the phrase "the myth of redemptive violence." With his wife, June Keener Wink, he held workshops around the world that combined religious-themed pottery, dancing, and biblical interpretation. Wink died in 2012 from complications of dementia.